LOW CHOLESTEROL

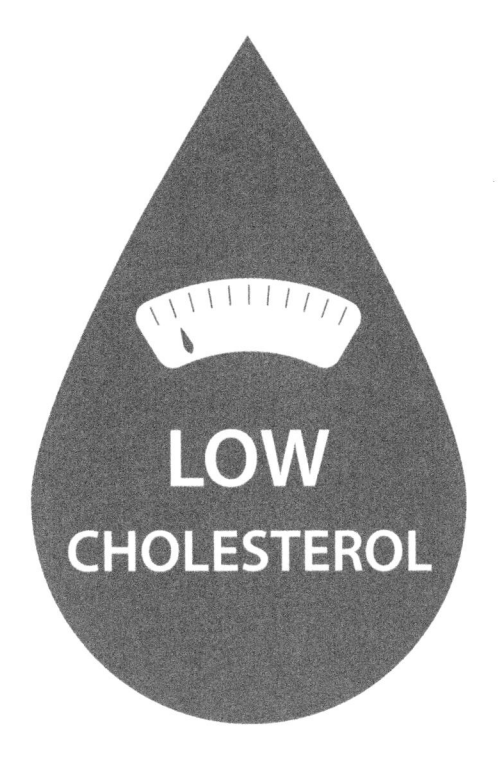

COOKBOOK FOR BEGINNERS

DISCOVER HOW TO KEEP YOUR CHOLESTEROL LEVELS UNDER CONTROL WITH 1000 DAYS OF HEALTHY RECIPES. INCLUDING A 28-DAY MEAL PLAN AND USEFUL EXERCISES

Jennifer Henderson

© **Copyright 2023 – Jennifer Henderson-All rights reserved.**

The content contained within this book may not be reproduced, duplicated or transmitted without direct written permission from the author or the publisher.

Under no circumstances will any blame or legal responsibility be held against the publisher, or author, for any damages, reparation, or monetary loss due to the information contained within this book. Either directly or indirectly.

Legal Notice:

This book is copyright protected. This book is only for personal use. You cannot amend, distribute, sell, use, quote or paraphrase any part, or the content within this book, without the consent of the author or publisher.

Disclaimer Notice:

Please note the information contained within this document is for educational and entertainment purposes only. All effort has been executed to present accurate, up to date, and reliable, complete information. No warranties of any kind are declared or implied. Readers acknowledge that the author is not engaging in the rendering of legal, financial, medical or professional advice. The content within this book has been derived from various sources. Please consult a licensed professional before attempting any techniques outlined in this book.

By reading this document, the reader agrees that under no circumstances is the author responsible for any losses, direct or indirect, which are incurred as a result of the use of information contained within this document, including, but not limited to, — errors, omissions, or inaccuracies.

Table of Contents

INTRODUCTION 8
CHAPTER 1: WHAT IS CHOLESTEROL? 9
   TYPES OF CHOLESTEROL 10
      LDL or LOW-DENSITY LIPOPROTEIN Cholesterol (Bad Cholesterol) 10
      HDL OR High-density Lipoprotein Cholesterol (good cholesterol) 10
      Normal Cholesterol Levels 11
   HOW DOES HIGH CHOLESTEROL AFFECT YOUR HEALTH? 11
CHAPTER 2: CAUSE AND SYMPTOMS 13
   CAUSES 13
   SYMPTOMS OF HIGH CHOLESTEROL 13
CHAPTER 3: BENEFITS OF A HEALTHY DIET AND REGULAR EXERCISE ON CHOLESTEROL LEVELS 15
   EXERCISE TO LOWERS CHOLESTEROL 16
CHAPTER 4: FOOD TO AVOID AND TO FOCUS ON 19
   FOODS TO EAT 19
   FOODS TO AVOID 21
CHAPTER 5: BREAKFAST AND SMOOTHIES RECIPES 24
   EGGPLANT FRIES 24
   LEMON BROCCOLI 25
   MILLET PORRIDGE 26
   QUINOA ALMOND PORRIDGE 27
   BELL PEPPER PANCAKES 28
   COCONUT-BERRY SUNRISE SMOOTHIE 29
   CREAMY CHOCOLATE-CHERRY SMOOTHIE 30
   EASY STRAWBERRY KIWI SMOOTHIE 31
   FRUIT SMOOTHIE WITH GREEK YOGURT 32
   GINGER AND CARROT PEAR SMOOTHIE 33
   GREEN APPLE AND OAT BRAN SMOOTHIE 34
   GREEN SMOOTHIE WITH BERRIES AND BANANA 35
   MUESLI WITH BERRIES, SEEDS, AND NUTS 36
   BERRY, WALNUT, AND CINNAMON QUINOA BOWL 37
   PEACH-CRANBERRY SUNRISE MUESLI 38
   CREAMY OATS BANANA PORRIDGE 39

CHAPTER 6: SALADS AND SIDES RECIPES 40

- Avocado and Watermelon Mix 40
- Rainbow Fruit Salad 41
- Cashew Pesto & Parsley with Veggies 42
- Cauliflower Sprinkled with Curry 43
- Celery and Chili Peppers Stir Fry 44
- Chicken and Quinoa Salad 45
- Chipotle Lime Avocado Salad 47
- Edamame and Avocado Dip 48
- Healthy Carrot Chips 49
- Homemade Guacamole 50
- Honey-Lime Berry Salad 51
- Nuts and Seeds Trail Mix 52
- Pita Chips 53
- Roasted Broccoli Salad 54
- Sweet and Spicy Brussels Sprouts 55
- Sautéed Garlic Mushrooms 56
- Smoky Cauliflower 57
- Sweet Carrots 58
- Tofu with Brussels Sprouts 59
- Tomato, Basil and Cucumber Salad 60
- Turmeric Peppers Platter 62
- Zucchini Pizza Bites 63

CHAPTER 7: SOUP AND STEWS RECIPES 64

- Collard Greens Dish 64
- Cauliflower and Horseradish Soup 65
- Chickpea Garlic Noodle Soup 67
- Cream of Mushroom Soup 68
- Curry Lentil Soup 70
- Flavors Vegetable Stew 71
- Greek Lentil Soup 73
- Hearty Vegetable Stew 74
- Indian Vegetable Stew 76
- Lentil Veggie Stew 78
- Mexican Lentil Soup 79
- Portobello Mushroom Stew 80
- Root Vegetable Stew 82
- Savory Chicken and Watermelon Rind Soup 83
- Spicy Lentil Chili 84
- Thick & Creamy Potato Soup 85
- Tuscan Fish Stew 86

CHAPTER 8: POULTRY RECIPES 88
Asian Chicken Breasts 88
Chicken Thighs and Apples Mix 89
Chicken Tikka 90
Chicken Tortillas 91
Classic Chicken Cooking with Tomatoes & Tapenade 92
Delicious Chicken Tenders 93
Garlic Mushroom Chicken 94
Grilled Chicken 95
Healthy Chicken Orzo 96
Hot Chicken Wings 98
Juicy Chicken Patties 99
Spicy Chicken 100
Tasty Chicken Wings 101

CHAPTER 9: PORK AND MEAT RECIPES 103
Beef Veggie Pot Meal 103
Beef with Mushrooms 104
Braised Beef Shanks 105
Citrus Pork 106
Easy Veal Chops 107
Garlic Lime Marinated Pork Chops 108
Grilled Fennel-Cumin Lamb Chops 109
Healthy Beef Cabbage 110
Healthy Meatballs 111
Hearty Pork Belly Casserole 112
Jerk Beef and Plantain Kabobs 113
Lamb Chops with Rosemary 114
Pork Meatloaf 115
Pork, Water Chestnuts, and Cabbage Salad 116
Ravaging Beef Pot Roast 117
Tasty Pork Patties 118

CHAPTER 10: SEAFOOD RECIPES. 120
Baked Fish Served with Vegetables 120
Baked Salmon with Dill 'N Garlic 121
Cilantro Lime Salmon Bowls 122
Easy Shrimp 123
Flounder with Tomatoes and Basil 125
Garlic and Tomatoes on Mussels 126
Ginger Sesame Salmon 127
Green Goddess Crab Salad with Endive 128

GRILLED HALIBUT AND FRUIT SALSA 129
PAN-GRILLED FISH STEAKS 130
PESTO SHRIMP PASTA 131
SALMON AVOCADO SALAD 132
SALMON WITH DILL AND LEMON 134
SALMON WRAP 135
SHRIMP AND AVOCADO SALAD 136
SIMPLE TUNA AND CUCUMBER SALAD 137
ROASTED VEGGIE AND LEMON PEPPER SALMON 138
STIR-FRIED SESAME SHRIMP 139

CHAPTER 11: VEGAN AND VEGETARIAN RECIPES 141

ALMOND NOODLES WITH CAULIFLOWER 141
BLACK BEANS BURGERS 142
BUCKWHEAT WITH POTATOES AND KALE 144
BUTTERNUT SQUASH, LENTILS, AND SPINACH GRATIN 145
CAULIFLOWER MASHED "POTATOES" 147
CAULIFLOWER, SPINACH, AND SWEET POTATO LASAGNA 148
CAULIFLOWER-CREAM PASTA WITH MINT 150
CHICKPEA BOWLS WITH TAHINI SAUCE 151
EASY BASIC TABLE SALAD 153
GARLIC LOVERS HUMMUS 154
GRILLED CAULIFLOWER WITH SPICY LENTIL SAUCE 155
HEALTHY CAULIFLOWER PURÉE 156
BASIL PESTO 157
PAN FRIED GREEN BEANS 158
ROASTED CHICKPEAS 159
ROASTED EGGPLANT SANDWICHES 160
SLOW COOKED QUINOA AND LENTILS TACOS 161
STUFFED TEX-MEX BAKED POTATOES 162
WHITE BEANS WITH SPINACH AND PAN-ROASTED TOMATOES 163
CORIANDER FALAFEL 164
CHEESY ZUCCHINI PANCAKE 166
HEARTY BRUSSELS AND PISTACHIO 167

CHAPTER 12: DESSERTS 169

ALMOND RICE PUDDING WITH RASPBERRY SAUCE 169
BANANA CREAM AND LOW-FAT YOGURT 170
BERRIES COBBLER 171
CHOCOLATE CHIP COOKIES 173
CHOCOLATE CUPCAKES 174
CINNAMON BAKED APPLE CHIPS 176

- Dates Cream 177
- Homemade protein Bar 178
- Shortbread Cookies 179
- Walnut Butter Bars 180
- Carrot Cake 181
- Mango Panna Cotta 183
- Strawberries and Amaretto Cream 184

CHAPTER 13: A 28-DAY MEAL PLAN 185

CHAPTER 14: WEEKLY PLANS OF SIMPLE EXERCISES 190

- **EXERCISES** explaination 190
- Lunges 190
- Jumping Jacks 190
- Squats 191
- Burpees 191
- Planks 191
- Pushups 192
- Crunches 193
- Twisting mountain climbers 193
- Side planks 194
- Sit-ups 194
- Glute Bridge 194
- FIRST WEEKLY WORKOUT PLAN 196
- SECOND WEEKLY WORKOUT PLAN 197

MEASURING CONVERSION TABLE FROM AMERICAN TO EUROPEAN 199

CONCLUSION 200

INDEX 201

INTRODUCTION

Having high blood cholesterol increases the risk of heart disease and stroke. In the United States, they are the leading cause of death, with 28.7 percent of deaths. Thousands of people are diagnosed with high cholesterol yearly, which raises the risk of circulatory problems, heart disease, and strokes. If you're reading this, chances are you or a family member is one of them. Perhaps you are at risk and want to avoid diseases associated with high cholesterol. Knowing which foods reduce cholesterol to make a balanced daily menu is simple enough. It is the first and most important step in the fight against diseases of the cardiovascular system.

Many people are afraid of cholesterol, but it isn't all bad. You can do numerous things to keep your cholesterol under control and healthy. The good news is that lowering your cholesterol is simple. This book will look at the various types of cholesterol and explain what they are and what they do for the body. It will also examine some causes and symptoms of high cholesterol and how to manage diabetes. This book is a great place to start if you have high cholesterol and want to lower it.

Learning to cook with less cholesterol is a good way to prepare healthy meals for your family that contain less saturated fat and fewer calories while retaining the flavor you crave. The good news is that it isn't as difficult as you may believe. There are simple methods for lowering the amount of cholesterol in your diet. You'll also learn the distinction between LDL and HDL cholesterol and why it's important to understand.

You can follow a healthy diet with less or no fat and cholesterol by eating organic products, taking fish oil supplements, exercising for 2 minutes daily, five days per week, and avoiding fast food. If you have high triglycerides, your doctor may prescribe medication as another option for lowering your cholesterol levels.

Before modifying your diet or adding exercise, consult your doctor, as with any health and nutrition recommendations. You'll have a better chance of living a healthy life if you eat a balanced diet, exercise regularly, and don't smoke. Let's get started

CHAPTER 1: WHAT IS CHOLESTEROL?

Cholesterol is a fatty molecule found in your bloodstream. Although your body requires it to produce healthy cells, high levels in the blood may increase your risk of heart disease. If we have too much cholesterol, some may become stuck in the artery walls and obstruct our blood vessels. When this happens, the blood may not supply enough oxygen to the heart.

Plants do not contain cholesterol.

Cholesterol is required by the body to produce hormones and steroids, as well as cell membranes. It is essential to survive.

The amount of cholesterol in our bodies, and the balance of the two types of cholesterol and other molecules like homocysteine, triglycerides, and free radicals, can predict whether we are at risk for atherosclerosis, heart disease, and stroke.

It's critical to consume good fat in the right amounts. Many recipes in this book have less than 100 mg of cholesterol.

Your blood arteries may develop fatty deposits as a result of high cholesterol. With time, these deposits build up, making it more difficult for enough blood to flow through your arteries. A sudden rupture of these deposits that produce a clot can cause a heart attack or stroke.

High cholesterol may be inherited, but it is more typically the consequence of poor lifestyle choices, making it both avoidable and curable. High cholesterol may be reduced by a nutritious diet, frequent exercise, and, in some cases, medication.

It is also obtained from animal products such as egg yolks, beef, and whole-milk dairy products. Too much cholesterol in the blood may cause plaque on blood vessel walls, obstruct blood flow to tissues and organs, and raise the risk of heart disease and stroke.

TYPES OF CHOLESTEROL

When discussing cholesterol, it is necessary to make a distinction because there are two main lipoproteins: low-intensity lipoproteins, denoted by the acronym LDL, and high-density lipoproteins, denoted by the acronym HDL. The first is "bad" cholesterol because they transport excess cholesterol from the liver to the arteries, whereas the second is "good" cholesterol because they remove cholesterol from the blood, protecting both the heart and the blood vessels. As a result, the cholesterol measured by blood tests can be summarized as a sum of LDL and HDL.

LDL OR LOW-DENSITY LIPOPROTEIN CHOLESTEROL (BAD CHOLESTEROL)

LDL is a vital lipoprotein that transports cholesterol in the blood throughout the body. However, most people have LDL levels that are too high, which are likely to accumulate within the walls of blood vessels where it is trapped and modified: this represents the beginning of the formation of a so-called "atherosclerotic plaque." These plaques can form in any blood vessel, including the heart, legs, and brain. The more cholesterol trapped in the plaque, the worse it gets. It can cause symptoms such as "angina" (chest discomfort) during exercise if it grows large enough to block blood flow in heart vessels partially. A heart attack is caused by a completely blocked artery that supplies blood to the heart. It is the leading cause of death in Western countries.

Extremely high LDL cholesterol levels (> 190 mg/dl; > 5 nmol/l) should prompt a second opinion, as familial hypercholesterolemia is possible. LDL cholesterol can be reduced by 10-15% through lifestyle changes. Medications such as statins or PCSK9 inhibitors may be prescribed if this is insufficient to achieve baseline values.

HDL OR HIGH-DENSITY LIPOPROTEIN CHOLESTEROL (GOOD CHOLESTEROL)

Although high HDL levels were previously associated with lower heart and vascular disease incidence, this view has shifted in recent years. HDL values alone do not indicate the quality of HDL cholesterol. Furthermore, studies show that increasing HDL levels with medications does not reduce heart disease. As a result, HDL levels, including so-called "ratios" in which high HDL levels may offset high LDL levels, should not be used to assess risk.

NORMAL CHOLESTEROL LEVELS

Blood experts say total cholesterol levels should be below 200 mg per deciliter. LDL cholesterol levels should ideally not exceed 100 mg/dl, but levels below 160 mg/dl are considered normal. Finally, HDL cholesterol levels should equal or exceed 50 mg/dl[1,2]. Total cholesterol levels in the blood are considered "moderately high" between 200 and 239 mg/dl and "high" when they reach or exceed 240 mg/dl. LDL cholesterol concentration, on the other hand, is considered "near-optimal" for values between 100 and 129 mg/dl, "moderately high" for values between 130 and 159 mg/dl, "high" for values between 160 and 189 mg/dl, and "very high" for values greater than 190 mg/dl. HDL cholesterol levels in the blood are considered "low" when they are less than 40 mg/dl and "high" when they are equal to or greater than 60 mg/dl[2].

HOW DOES HIGH CHOLESTEROL AFFECT YOUR HEALTH?

The primary reason why having too much LDL cholesterol in your blood is bad for your health has to do with a process known as atherosclerosis, which can be simply thought of as plaque buildup in your arteries. Your arteries are the blood vessels that carry fresh, oxygenated blood to your organs from your heart. Having chronically high LDL cholesterol levels are among the many contributing factors to plaque formation in the bloodstream.

A healthy body requires healthy arteries, but they are extraordinarily sensitive to damage, which may occur over time due to aging, improper diet, and lifestyle factors. The formation of plaque ultimately increases your risk of various cardiovascular conditions because they narrow and harden your arteries, restricting blood flow. This restricted oxygen flow to your vital organs can cause life-threatening cardiovascular issues.

The table below shows normal lipogram ranges.

Age group	Total cholesterol (mg/dL[a])	Non-HDL (mg/dL)	LDL (mg/dL)	HDL (mg/dL)
0–19	<170	<120	<100	>45
20 and above (Male)	125–200	<130	<100	≥40
20 and above (Female)	125–200	<130	<100	≥50

[a] milligrams per deciliter of blood

CHAPTER 2: CAUSE AND SYMPTOMS

CAUSES

Both genetic and dietary factors cause cholesterol. You would also have high cholesterol if your parents or grandparents had high cholesterol. Physicians are unsure whether the increased risk is due to genetics or if individuals who inherit unhealthy eating habits prefer to eat the same way, implying that even inherited risk may be partially due to diet.

Nutrition, on the other hand, plays a significant role in cholesterol levels. The main issue in our diets is saturated fat. Unfortunately, many popular foods, such as fatty meats, fried meals, high-fat dairy products such as whole milk, cream, and cheese made from whole milk, and commercial baked goods are high in saturated fats.

Normally, these occurrences do not occur until plaque builds up in your arteries due to high cholesterol levels. Plaque can narrow arteries, allowing less blood to flow through. Plaque alters the structure of your artery lining, which can have serious consequences.

SYMPTOMS OF HIGH CHOLESTEROL

High cholesterol does not always cause symptoms. Most of the time, it only leads to emergencies. Excessive cholesterol, for example, can result in a heart attack or stroke.

Over time you may experience chest pain, which could lead to a heart attack. This condition is more common in men over 45 and women over 55. Heart attacks are also increased by unhealthy habits such as smoking, overeating, and lack of physical activity.

Your elevated LDL cholesterol levels can only be determined through a blood test. Untreated cholesterol can eventually cause plaque to build, weaken the heart, and increase your chance of heart attack or stroke. Watch for indications of a heart attack or an impending stroke, such as:

- Nausea

- Numbness
- Flustered speech
- Extreme exhaustion
- Angina, or chest pain
- Breathing problems
- Numbness or coldness to the extremities
- Hypertension (high blood pressure)

Do not hesitate to visit the nearby 24-hour emergency hospital if you are concerned about your symptoms. They could analyze your blood work and do tests to ensure nothing is wrong.

Learn about the blood tests that are carried out at the emergency room.

How can you determine whether you have high cholesterol without a blood test?

Unless you are experiencing a medical emergency or know the blood test results, you cannot tell if you have high cholesterol. Depending on the gender, lipid testing should start between 9 and 11 and continue every five years until age 45 or 55.

CHAPTER 3: BENEFITS OF A HEALTHY DIET AND REGULAR EXERCISE ON CHOLESTEROL LEVELS

To make sure you're receiving enough calories while following the low-cholesterol diet, start with 2,000 calories per day. This amount will increase as you lose weight, so be aware of how many calories you take and modify it as necessary.

In addition to consuming a range of healthy meals, it's important to stay hydrated and exercise frequently. The low-cholesterol diet's exercise component will use much more energy than a typical diet but will help you lose weight rapidly. Exercise improves healthy skin and hair as well as weight reduction.

A variety of factors influence your cholesterol and overall heart health. Some of these, such as genetics and age, are uncontrollable. Others, on the other hand, believe you. When it comes down to it, there are three ways to lower cholesterol. One option is to consult with your doctor about medication. Another option is to exercise. Studies have shown that regular exercise lowers cholesterol and the risk of heart disease and stroke. Many cardiologists recommend at least 30 minutes of daily walking. It isn't difficult, but it does require commitment.

A low-cholesterol diet focuses solely on lowering cholesterol in the blood. To be classified as low-cholesterol, a person must consume less cholesterol-rich food while avoiding foods high in fat and saturated fat. The goal is to lower LDL (low-density lipoprotein) or bad cholesterol levels in the blood while increasing HDL (high-density lipoprotein) or good cholesterol levels. For example, a person may consume more vegetables, fruits, and whole grains while avoiding red meat and eggs due to their high cholesterol content.

The first goal of a low-cholesterol diet is to reduce the amount of cholesterol the liver produces. Because the liver produces a large amount of cholesterol each day, it is critical to maintaining a healthy diet to avoid excess amounts. Fast and fried foods high in saturated fats, such as doughnuts and French fries, are the main causes of elevated blood cholesterol levels.

The doctor may prescribe drugs if diet-reducing cholesterol is insufficient to alleviate the problem. There are specific types of drugs known as statins (Lipitor and atorvastatin). Statins reduce cholesterol by interrupting the production of cholesterol in the liver. The main side-effect of statin drugs is muscle pain which can be reduced by lowering the dose or changing it to another statin with fewer side effects. Another group of drugs that can lower cholesterol levels is bile acid sequestrants, such as colesevelam, which works by binding bile acids in the intestine and preventing them from being reabsorbed into the body.

Because the liver produces most cholesterol, any diet low in fat can result in a fatty liver. The doctor may prescribe an anti-fat pill to help with these disorders. Furthermore, some cholesterol-lowering medications for the heart and blood vessels may cause gastrointestinal distress, such as diarrhea or constipation. If you have been taking statins, you should be monitored because blood tests may show that you still have elevated cholesterol levels in your blood despite changing your diet.

Reducing your risk of developing heart disease is the main advantage of lowering cholesterol through the diet. Reduced artery hardening can help prevent or delay coronary artery disease by lowering bad cholesterol and increasing good (HDL) cholesterol. Hypertension, also known as high blood pressure, is associated with high levels of bad cholesterol and triglycerides. High blood pressure increases the risk of strokes, heart attacks, and kidney failure. These conditions can be improved by lowering bad cholesterol.

EXERCISE TO LOWERS CHOLESTEROL

While many individuals know the value of exercise in enhancing health, many are unaware of how it helps lower HDL while raising LDL levels. Your body may increase its HDL level simply by engaging in aerobic activity, which is necessary to shield you from significant medical illnesses like heart disease.

It's crucial to exercise. Exercising boosts the heart and helps people lose weight. You should commit to moderate exercise daily for 60 minutes to reduce weight.

Cardiovascular workouts include jogging, dancing, swimming, gardening, aerobics, and brisk walking.

Certain instruments, according to nutritionists, are needed. First, physical activity raises the enzymes that aid in moving LDL from circulation to the liver. Either bile or feces are produced from the cholesterol. As a result, your LDL will decrease the more physical activity you do.

Second, physical activity enlarges the protein molecules that carry cholesterol throughout the body. While certain substances are huge and fleecy, others are thick and tiny. The dense, microscopic particles can enter the coats of the heart and blood arteries, making them more harmful than the fluffy, huge particles. Yet according to recent studies, physical activity can enlarge the protein components of poor and healthy lipoproteins.

So, even a tiny amount of activity is preferable to none; nevertheless, the more exercise, the better.

The American Heart Association recommends engaging in physical exercise for an average of 40 minutes, three or four times a week, to lower cholesterol levels, lowering blood pressure, and reduce your risk of stroke and heart attack. The American Heart Association advises getting at least 212 hours of moderate or 114 hours of vigorous exercise weekly for overall cardiovascular health. If you'd like, you can alternate between strong and moderate activities.

Moderate workout examples include:

- Jogging or jogging on a treadmill
- Climbing and hiking uphill
- Riding a bicycle
- Playing sports like tennis or basketball
- Working around the house, like gardening.
- Swimming, aerobic dance, tennis, biking, and other sports

The simplest approach to determine if you are working out at a healthy level is to take a test. According to the American Heart Association, you must be able to carry on a conversation while engaging in moderate exercise and pause after speaking if engaging in strenuous activity.

Use specialized equipment or just your fingertips to check if your heart rate is at your target level. Subtract your age from 220 to determine your maximal heart rate. The ideal heart rate ranges from 50% to 85%.

CHAPTER 4: FOOD TO AVOID AND TO FOCUS ON

FOODS TO EAT

Eat More Fiber

There are two types of dietary fiber: soluble fiber and insoluble fiber. Because it dissolves in water, soluble fiber is beneficial for lowering LDL cholesterol levels. It works in the intestines by absorbing bile salts. The body removes cholesterol from the circulation to produce additional bile salts. Every day, 5 to 10 grams of soluble fiber should be consumed.

Eat Healthy Fats

Doctors agree that a diet high in healthy fats is preferable to one low in fat. The healthiest fats to consume are monounsaturated fats. You should consume extra-virgin olive oil, unrefined safflower oil, almonds, and avocados. Omega-3 fatty acids, found in walnuts, tofu, soybeans, fatty fish, and flaxseed, are good fats to eat. Most Americans are deficient in omega-3 fats and consume too much omega-6 fat in polyunsaturated oils.

While you want to keep fat intake modest to maintain your ideal weight, oils like olive and canola may help decrease cholesterol levels. They are high in polyunsaturated fat, the healthiest kind of fat.

Oatmeal

It's simple to start your new low-cholesterol diet by having a bowl of oats or cold cereal for breakfast. Around 1 to 2 grams of soluble fiber are included in oats. Add slices of banana or berries to make it more delicious. 20 to 35 grams of fiber per day are recommended, including at least 5 to 10 grams of soluble fiber.

Barley and Other Whole Grains

Oatmeal, barley, and other whole grain diets reduce the risk of heart problems, usually by providing soluble fiber.

Fish

Omega-3 fatty acids are found in fish oils and help prevent blood vessel blockages and clots. According to medical experts, fish should be consumed at least twice weekly.

Soy

Compounds in soy protein, such as those found in tofu, soybeans, and soy-based dairy substitutes, cause blood arteries to dilate, allowing the body to receive the required blood. Antioxidants are also present, which have been shown to lower the risk of cancer and heart disease.

Nuts

Nuts, like fish, are high in omega-3 fatty acids. However, since they are high in calories, you should have them in moderation.

Beans

Soluble fiber is particularly abundant in beans. You will feel satisfied longer because digesting takes the body a while. For this reason, beans are a healthy food for people who desire to lose weight. Beans are a relaxed meal with various options and preparation methods for your diet.

Okra and Eggplant

You should include these two low-calorie veggies in your diet since they are excellent providers of soluble fiber.

Fruits like apples, strawberries, grapes, and citrus

These fruits contain a lot of pectins, a soluble fiber that reduces LDL.

Soy

Consuming soybeans and products from them, such as soy milk and tofu, were formerly hailed as effective methods for lowering blood cholesterol levels. Research reveals that it has a more subdued impact on the body, with a daily intake of 25 grams of soy protein lowering LDL by 5% to 6%.

Fruits and vegetables

These are good for us because of their high fiber and low-fat content. Fiber helps to decrease the amount of cholesterol absorbed by our bodies, while fat adds more to it.

FOODS TO AVOID

Red Meats

Ground beef, ribs, pork chops, beef roast, and steak are all high in cholesterol and saturated fat.

Choose 90% lean ground beef, lean beef cuts like sirloin, tenderloin, filet or flank steak, pork loin, or tenderloin, and lower-fat animal protein options such as baked skinless or lean ground chicken.

Salt

High blood pressure may be a result of excessive salt consumption. You know the negative health effects of canned soup and salty snacks. But did you know it may also be discovered in fast food sandwiches, cold cuts, cured meats, pizza, and bread and rolls?

You might be surprised by how frequently it appears in frozen food. Always read the labeling if in doubt. Limit your daily dose to 2,300–2,400 mg.

Sugar

Indeed, it is delicious. Nevertheless, consuming too much might result in weight gain, diabetes, heart disease, and cholesterol issues. Of course, this is easier said than done, so try to control your intake.

You'll know many "usual suspects," like ice cream, soda, sweet tea, sweets, cakes, and cookies. But did you realize that unexpected meals like fast food and spaghetti sauce contain sugar? This category has many tomatoes, ketchup, breakfast bars, and tonic. The first three to five elements should be your main attention because they are listed by weight, from most to least significant. Avoid prepared meals that list one ingredient, and read the full box. Consult your doctor.

Egg Yolks

214 mg of cholesterol, or more than two-thirds of the daily allowance, may be found in one egg yolk. Use egg whites instead of whole eggs if you can't manufacture an egg substitute.

The cholesterol in eggs is misunderstood. One egg has just 8% saturated fat but over 60% of the recommended daily cholesterol intake. Eggs are high in protein, low in calories, and packed with anti-inflammatory minerals, B vitamins, and iron. Egg whites, which are strong in protein but low in cholesterol, should be your only choice if you need to reduce your cholesterol consumption.

Saturated Fats

Saturated fats primarily cause high cholesterol levels. Saturated fats, in general, are solid fats at room temperature. Saturated fats are classified into many types, and the amount of saturated fat in packaged goods in the United States is listed on the nutrition information label. It implies that you have complete control over the amount of saturated fat you eat. The American Heart Association and others recommend consuming no more than 20 grams of saturated fat daily. The recipes in this book will guide you to the cuts of meat and cooking techniques necessary to achieve your goal.

Poultry Skin

Although poultry skin may not contain as much saturated fat as red meat, it still does. A chicken thigh with the skin has about 2 g more saturated fat than one with only the meat. And in this case, losing the fat is easy—avoid eating the skin.

Whole-Milk Dairy

Dairy products are another category where making informed choices may lower saturated fat intake. Avoid full milk or cream-based products, and choose fat-free sour cream, cream cheese, skim milk, and reduced-fat cheeses. Instead of cream, use fat-free evaporated milk.

Foods that are processed and contain trans-fat, artificial butter flavor, partially hydrogenated oil, or shortening

Carbonated beverages like soda as they are full of carbohydrates and sugar, which can increase your LDL cholesterol levels. Even diet soft drinks contain phosphoric acid, increasing the risk of kidney stone formation.

Processed foods like commercial soups, frozen dinners, etc., as they contain unhealthy fat, preservatives, and flavor enhancers. These foods also lack the necessary nutrients and vitamins.

Slices of bread made from refined flour are high in calories, trans fat, saturated fat, and cholesterol. These pieces of bread can cause an increase in triglyceride levels and can clog the arteries.

Starchy vegetables like potatoes, corn, etc., high in carbohydrates, can cause weight gain if consumed regularly.

CHAPTER 5: BREAKFAST AND SMOOTHIES RECIPES

EGGPLANT FRIES

Prep 15 minutes | **Cooking Time** 15 minutes | **Serving** 4 Persons

Ingredients:

- 2 egg
- 2 cup almond flour
- 2 tbsp coconut oil, spray
- 2 eggplants, peeled and cut thinly
- Salt and pepper

Directions:

1. Preheat your oven to 400°F.
2. Take a bowl and mix with salt and black pepper in it.
3. Take another bowl and beat eggs until frothy.
4. Dip the eggplant pieces into the eggs.
5. Then coat them with the flour mixture.
6. Add another layer of flour and an egg.
7. Then, take a baking sheet and grease it with coconut oil on top.
8. Bake for about 15 minutes

Nutrition: Calories: 1430, Fat: 115,0 g, Carbs: 23,4 g, Protein: 75,5 g, Cholesterol: 360 mg

LEMON BROCCOLI

Prep
10 minutes

Cooking Time
15 minutes

Serving
4 Persons

Ingredients:

- 2 heads broccoli, separated into florets
- 2 tsp extra-virgin olive oil
- 1 tsp sea salt
- ½ tsp pepper
- 1 garlic clove, minced
- ½ tsp lemon juice

Directions:

1. Set your oven to 400°F for preparation.
2. Broccoli florets should be placed in a big bowl with extra virgin olive oil, pepper, sea salt, and garlic.
3. Spread the broccoli on a fine baking sheet in a single, equal layer.
4. Bake for 15-20 minutes in your preheated oven or until the florets are soft enough to penetrate with a fork.
5. Before serving, liberally squeeze lemon juice over the vegetables.

6. Enjoy!

Nutrition: Calories: 354, Fat: 13,8 g, Carbs: 30,2 g, Protein: 27,5 g, Cholesterol: 0 mg

MILLET PORRIDGE

Prep 10 minutes | **Cooking Time** 15 minutes | **Serving** 4

Ingredients:

- 1 cup millet, rinsed and drained
- A pinch salt
- 3 cup water
- 2 tbsp almonds, chopped finely
- 6-8 drops liquid stevia
- 1 cup unsweetened almond milk
- 2 tbsp fresh blueberries

Directions:

1. Add the millet over medium-low heat in a nonstick pan and cook for about 3 minutes, stirring continuously.
2. Add the salt and water and stir to combine
3. Increase the heat to medium and bring it to a boil.
4. Cook for about 15 minutes.

5. Stir in the almonds, stevia, and almond milk and cook for 5 minutes.

6. Top with the blueberries and serve.

Nutrition: Calories: 1789, Fat: 54,9 g, Carbs 305,6 g, Sugar 7,8 g, Fiber 37,1 g, Protein 17,8 g, Cholesterol: 0 mg

QUINOA ALMOND PORRIDGE

Prep
10 minutes

Cooking Time
15 minutes

Serving
4

Ingredients:

- 2 cups water
- 1 cup dry quinoa, rinsed
- ½ tsp organic vanilla extract
- ½ cup unsweetened almond milk
- 10-12 drops liquid stevia
- ¼ tsp lemon peel, grated freshly
- ½ tsp ground cinnamon
- ½ tsp ground nutmeg
- A pinch ground cloves
- 1 cup fresh mixed berries

Directions:

1. Mix the water, quinoa, and vanilla essence in a pan over low heat and cook for about 15 minutes, stirring occasionally.

2. Stir in the almond milk, stevia, lemon peel, and spices, and remove from the heat.

3. Top with the berries and serve warm.

Nutrition: Calories: 788, Fat: 14,7 g, Carbs: 132,8 g, Sugar: 10,2 g, Fiber: 16,3 g, Protein: 28,0 g, Cholesterol: 0 mg

BELL PEPPER PANCAKES

Prep
10 minutes

Cooking Time
15 minutes

Serving
4

Ingredients:

- ½ cup chickpea flour
- ¼ tsp baking powder
- A pinch sea salt
- A pinch red pepper flakes, crushed
- ½ cup plus 2 tbsp filtered water
- ¼ cup green bell peppers, seeded and chopped finely
- ¼ cup scallion, chopped finely
- 2 tsp olive oil

Directions:

1. Mix flour, baking powder, salt, and red pepper flakes in a bowl.
2. Add the water and mix until well combined.
3. Fold in bell pepper and scallion.
4. In a large frying pan, heat the oil over low heat.
5. Add half the mixture and cook for 1-2 minutes per side.

6. Repeat with the remaining mixture.

7. Serve warm.

Nutrition: Calories: 274, Fat: 12,5 g, Carbs: 28,7 g, Sugar: 6 g, Fiber: 7,8 g, Protein: 11,7 g, Cholesterol: 0 mg

COCONUT-BERRY SUNRISE SMOOTHIE

Prep
10 minutes

Cooking Time
0 minutes

Serving
4

Ingredients:

- ½ cup mixed berries (blueberries, strawberries, blackberries)
- 1 tbsp ground chia seeds
- 2 tbsp unsweetened coconut flakes
- ½ cup unsweetened plain almonds milk
- ½ cup lettuce
- ¼ cup unsweetened vanilla nonfat yogurt
- ½ cup ice

Directions:

1. Combine the berries, chia seeds, almond milk, coconut flakes, lettuce, yogurt, and ice in a blender jar.

2. Process until completely smooth. Serve.

Nutrition: Calories: 265, Fat: 13,3 g, Protein: 8,6 g, Carbs: 27,5 g, Sugar: 17,3 g, Fiber: 9,1 g, Sodium: 36 mg, Cholesterol: 1 mg

CREAMY CHOCOLATE-CHERRY SMOOTHIE

Prep
10 minutes

Cooking Time
0 minutes

Serving
4

Ingredients:

For the smoothie:

- ½ cup (120 ml) unsweetened vanilla almond or cashew milk
- 1 tsp vanilla extract
- 1 cup fresh baby spinach
- 1 tbsp almond butter
- 1 tbsp unsweetened cocoa powder
- ½ cup (120 ml) low-fat plain Greek yogurt
- ¾ cup frozen cherries
- ½ medium banana, sliced and frozen
- 3 to 4 ice cubes

For serving:

1. ¼ cup berries, such as blueberries, raspberries, or strawberries
2. ½ small banana, sliced
3. 1 tsp sliced almonds
4. ½ tbsp cacao nibs

Directions:

1. Combine the spinach, milk, vanilla, almond butter, yogurt, cocoa, cherries, banana, and ice in a high-powered blender. Blend until thick and creamy.

2. Pour the mixture into a bowl and top with the sliced banana, berries, almonds, and cacao nibs. Serve.

Nutrition: Calories: 470, Fat: 16,4 g, Saturated fat: 3,29 g, Carbs: 58 g, Protein: 22,5 g, Fiber: 11,4 g, Sugar: 47,8 g, Cholesterol: 5 m

EASY STRAWBERRY KIWI SMOOTHIE

Prep
10 minutes

Cooking Time
0 minutes

Serving
4

Ingredients:

- 1 cup fresh strawberries
- 2 kiwi fruits, peeled and cut into quarters
- 1 cup unsweetened yogurt
- 1 cup low-fat plant-based milk

Directions:

1. Add strawberries, kiwi, yogurt, and milk to the blender. Blend on high until smooth.

2. Serve with fresh diced strawberries, kiwis, and straw as desired.

Nutrition: Calories: 282, Protein: 17,2 g, Fat: 5,6 g, Carbs: 40,5 g, Sodium: 166 mg, Fiber: 7,2 g, Sugar: 40,5 g, Cholesterol: 4 mg

FRUIT SMOOTHIE WITH GREEK YOGURT

Prep
10 minutes

Cooking Time
0 minutes

Serving
4

Ingredients:

- 1 cup (240 ml) almond milk
- 3 cups kale or spinach
- 1 small green apple
- ½ cup frozen peaches
- ¼ cup (60 ml) vanilla Greek yogurt
- 1 banana, peeled
- 1 orange, peeled

Directions:

1. Put all the ingredients in a blender in the order listed and blend thoroughly until smooth.
2. Serve.

Nutrition: Calories: 432, Fat: 10,8 g, Carbs: 71,4 g, Protein: 13 g, Cholesterol: 9 mg, Sodium: 115 mg, Fiber: 11.1 g

GINGER AND CARROT PEAR SMOOTHIE

Prep
10 minutes

Cooking Time
0 minutes

Serving
4

Ingredients:

- 2 carrots, peeled and grated
- 1 ripe pear, unpeeled, cored, and chopped
- 2 tsp grated fresh ginger
- 1 lime, juiced, and zest
- 1 cup water
- ½ tsp ground cinnamon
- ¼ tsp ground nutmeg

Directions:

1. Add the carrots, pear, ginger, lime juice, zest, water, cinnamon, and nutmeg, whirl until smooth, and let the blender run long enough, so the mixture is truly pureed.
2. Pour the mixture into two glasses and serve and enjoy.

Nutrition: Calories: 169, Fat: 2,3 g, Sodium: 196 mg, Carbs: 34 g, Sugar: 34 g, Fiber: 12,8 g, Protein: 3,4 g, Cholesterol: 0 m

GREEN APPLE AND OAT BRAN SMOOTHIE

Prep
10 minutes

Cooking Time
0 minutes

Serving
4

Ingredients:

- ¾ cup (180 ml) unsweetened almond or cashew milk
- 2 tbsp oat bran
- ¼ tsp apple pie spice or ground cinnamon
- ½ tsp vanilla extract
- 1 cup baby spinach or ⅓ cup frozen
- ½ cup (120 ml) low-fat plain Greek yogurt
- 1 tbsp avocado
- ½ medium banana, sliced and frozen
- ½ cup green apple, unpeeled, chopped, and frozen
- ¼ cup cooked or canned white beans, rinsed and drained
- ½ cup ice

Directions:

1. Mix the milk, oat bran, vanilla, spinach, apple pie spice, yogurt, banana, beans, avocado, and ice in a high-powered blender.
2. Blend until smooth.

Nutrition: Calories: 532, Fat: 17,4 g, Saturated fat: 2,18 g, Carbs: 67,1 g, Protein: 25 g, Cholesterol: 0

GREEN SMOOTHIE WITH BERRIES AND BANANA

Prep
10 minutes

Cooking Time
0 minutes

Serving
4

Ingredients:

- 2 cups spinach
- 1 tbsp almond butter
- ¾ cup frozen blackberries
- 1 cup water
- 1 small frozen banana, chopped
- ¾ cup frozen blueberries

Directions:

1. In a blender, put the spinach and water. Start mixing on low speed until the spinach begins to decompose, then turn on medium speed and stir until it is completely decomposed and smooth.

2. Put the blackberries, blueberries, banana, and almond butter, and start combining on medium-high speed for 1 minute until the desired consistency is reached.

3. Remove from the blender and enjoy.

Nutrition: Calories: 220, Fat: 6,5 g, Protein: 6,8 g, Carbs: 33,5 g, Fiber: 7,3 g, Sugar: 25,6 g, Sodium: 108 mg, Cholesterol: 0 mg

MUESLI WITH BERRIES, SEEDS, AND NUTS

Prep
5 minutes

Cooking Time
30 minutes

Serving
4

Ingredients:

- 1 cup rolled oats
- 1 cup sunflower seeds
- ½ cup chopped almonds
- A pinch salt to taste
- 1 tbsp extra-virgin olive oil
- 2 cups unsweetened almond milk
- 2 cups berries

Directions:

1. Preheat the oven to 300°F. Line a baking sheet with parchment paper.
2. Combine the oats, sunflower seeds, almonds, and salt on the prepared baking sheet. Mix well.
3. Drizzle with the oil, and stir well. Spread the mixture in a thin layer.
4. Transfer the baking sheet to the oven, stirring once halfway through, for 30 minutes or until the muesli is lightly browned. Remove from the oven.
5. Set aside to cool. Serve the muesli with almond milk and berries.

Nutrition: Calories: 1817; Fat: 105 g; Carbs: 164,7 g; Protein: 52,7 g, Cholesterol: 0 mg

BERRY, WALNUT, AND CINNAMON QUINOA BOWL

Prep
5 minutes

Cooking Time
20 minutes

Serving
2

Ingredients:

- ½ cup quinoa
- 1 cup unsweetened almond milk
- 1 tsp cinnamon, plus more for coating
- 10 raw walnuts
- 1 cup strawberries, sliced

Directions:

1. Preheat the oven to 425°F, and line a baking sheet with parchment paper. Bring the quinoa, almond milk, and cinnamon to a boil in a medium pot.

2. Low the heat to a simmer, then cover for 12 minutes or until the almond milk has been absorbed.

3. Put the walnuts and a dash of cinnamon onto the prepared baking sheet and bake for 5 minutes until lightly golden.

4. Combine the quinoa and walnuts in a serving bowl and top with the strawberries. (When storing, put the quinoa only in the refrigerator for up to 1 week. Add the walnuts and strawberries when ready to eat.)

Nutrition: Calories: 1074; Fat: 43,8 g; Carbs: 135,8 g; Protein: 34,2 g, Cholesterol: 0 mg

PEACH-CRANBERRY SUNRISE MUESLI

Prep: 10 minutes | **Cooking Time:** 0 minutes | **Serving:** 1

Ingredients:

- ⅓ cup vanilla soy milk
- 3 tbsp rolled oats
- 1 tbsp chia seeds
- 1 tbsp buckwheat (optional)
- 1 peach
- 1 tbsp dried cranberries
- 1 tbsp sunflower seeds

Directions:

1. Mix the soy milk, oats, chia seeds, and buckwheat (if using) in a large bowl. Soak for at least 10 minutes (and as long as overnight).
2. Meanwhile, cut the peach into bite-size pieces.
3. When the oats have softened up, sprinkle with the cranberries, sunflower seeds, and peach chunks.

Nutrition: Calories: 387; Fat: 13,2 g; Carbs: 52 g; Protein: 15,1 g, Cholesterol: 0 mg

CREAMY OATS BANANA PORRIDGE

Prep
10 minutes

Cooking Time
5 minutes

Serving
1

Ingredients:

- ¼ cup steel-cut oats
- 1 tbsp peanut butter
- ½ tsp vanilla
- ½ tbsp chia seeds
- ½ banana, mashed
- ½ cup unsweetened almond milk
- 1 cup water

Directions:

1. Add oats & water to a saucepan and bring to a boil.
2. Once oats thicken, add vanilla, chia seeds, mashed banana, and almond milk and cook over low heat for 5 minutes. Stir constantly.
3. Top with peanut butter and serve.

Nutrition: Calories: 357; Fat: 17,3 g; Carbs: 37.2 g; Protein: 13 g, Cholesterol: 0 mg

CHAPTER 6: SALADS AND SIDES RECIPES

AVOCADO AND WATERMELON MIX

Prep
10 minutes

Cooking Time
0 minutes

Serving
4

Ingredients:

- 1 ½ cup chopped tomatoes
- 1 ½ cup watermelon, cubed
- ½ Jalapeño, chopped
- A pinch salt and black pepper
- 1 avocado, peeled, pitted and cubed
- ½ tsp olive oil
- 2 tbsp ginger, grated
- 1 lime, zest and grated
- 2 tsp black sesame seeds
- 2 tbsp mint, chopped
- 3 tbsp lime juice

Directions:

1. In a salad bowl, combine the tomatoes with the watermelon, jalapeno, salt, pepper, avocado, oil, ginger, lime zest, black seeds, mint, and lime juice.

2. Toss, divide between plates and serve as a side dish.

Nutrition: Calories: 796; Fat: 71,3 g; Carbs: 21,6 g; Protein: 17,2 g, Cholesterol: 0 mg

RAINBOW FRUIT SALAD

Prep
10 minutes

Cooking Time
0 minutes

Serving
4

Ingredients:

For the Fruit Salad:

- 1-pound strawberries, hulled, sliced
- 1 cup kiwis, halved, cubed
- 1 ¼ cups blueberries
- 1 ⅓ cups blackberries
- 1 cup pineapple chunks

For the Maple Lime Dressing:

- 2 tsp lime zest
- ¼ cup maple syrup
- 1 tbsp lime juice

Directions:

1. Prepare the salad and for this, take a bowl, place all its ingredients, and toss until mixed.

2. Prepare the dressing, and for this; take a small bowl, place all its ingredients, and whisk well.

3. Drizzle the dressing over the salad, toss until coated, and serve.

Nutrition: Calories: 774, Fat: 5,9 g, Carbs: 166 g, Protein: 14 g, Fiber: 27,3 g, Cholesterol: 0 mg

CASHEW PESTO & PARSLEY WITH VEGGIES

Prep 15 minutes | **Cooking Time** 10 minutes | **Serving** 3

Ingredients:

- 3 zucchinis, sliced
- 8 bamboo skewers soaked in water
- 2 red peppers, sliced
- 2 tablespoons of olive oil
- 3 Eggplant
- 4 lemon wedges
- 1 cup couscous salad

Preparing the cashew pesto:

- ½ cup cashew (roasted)
- ½ cup parsley
- 2 cups grated parmesan

- 2 tbsp lime juice

Directions:

1. Cut the red pepper, eggplant, and zucchini at a desired size and toss with oil and salt and thread them onto the skewers.

2. Cook the bamboo sticks for 6-8 minutes on a barbecue grill pan on medium heat.

3. Also, grill the lemon wedges on both sides.

4. To prepare the cashew pesto, combine all ingredients in the food processor and blend.

5. For serving, place the grill skewers on a plate with the grilled lemon slices and drizzle some cashew pesto over the top.

Nutrition: Calories: 1468; Fat: 81 g; Carbs: 97,4 g; Protein: 87,6 g, Cholesterol: 0 mg

CAULIFLOWER SPRINKLED WITH CURRY

Prep 10 minutes | **Cooking Time** 60 minutes | **Serving** 4

Ingredients:

- 1 tbsp vegetable oil
- 1 cauliflower head, florets separated
- 2 carrots, sliced
- 1 red onion, chopped
- ¾ cup coconut milk
- ½ cup water.

- 2 garlic cloves, minced
- 2 tbsp curry powder
- A pinch salt and black pepper
- 1 tbsp red pepper flakes
- 1 tsp garam masala

Directions:

1. In a large pot, cook the onion and garlic with oil for about 5 minutes on medium heat. Once they start to brown, add the spices and the vegetables.
2. Cook for about 5 minutes at medium heat, then add the coconut milk and the water.
3. Put on low heat, cover, and cook for 1 hour, stirring occasionally, don't burn the bottom.
4. Once the liquid is thickened up, and the beg is cooked, turn off the heat and leave to rest for 20 minutes.
5. Divide into bowls and serve.

Nutrition: Calories: 560; Fat: 47,6 g; Carbs: 17,7 g; Protein: 13,3 g, Cholesterol: 0 m

CELERY AND CHILI PEPPERS STIR FRY

Prep 10 minutes   **Cooking Time** 5 minutes   **Serving** 6

Ingredients:

- 2 tbsp olive oil
- 3 chili peppers, dried and crushed

- 🧑‍🍳 4 cups julienned celery
- 🧑‍🍳 2 tbsp coconut aminos

Directions:

1. Heat a pan with the oil at medium-high heat, add chili peppers, stir, and cook them for 2 minutes.
2. Add the celery and the coconut aminos, stir and cook for 3 minutes.
3. Divide between plates and serve as a side dish.

Nutrition: Calories: 412; Fat: 41,3 g; Carbs: 5,8 g; Protein: 4,4 g, Cholesterol: 0 mg

CHICKEN AND QUINOA SALAD

Prep
10 minutes

Cooking Time
20 minutes

Serving
2

Ingredients:

- 🧑‍🍳 2 tbsp olive oil
- 🧑‍🍳 2 ounces quinoa
- 🧑‍🍳 2 ounces cherry tomatoes, cut in quarters
- 🧑‍🍳 3 ounces sweet corn
- 🧑‍🍳 1 lime, juiced
- 🧑‍🍳 1 lime zest, grated

- ♟ 2 spring onions, chopped
- ♟ A small red chili pepper, chopped
- ♟ 1 avocado
- ♟ 2 ounces chicken meat

Directions:

1. Fill water in a pan and bring it to a boil over a medium-high heat
2. Add quinoa, stir, and cook for 12 minutes.
3. Meanwhile, put the sweetcorn in a pan and heat over medium-high heat.
4. Cook for 5 minutes and leave aside for now.
5. Drain quinoa, transfer to a bowl, and add tomatoes, corn, coriander, onions, chili, lime zest, olive oil, and salt and black pepper to taste and toss.
6. In another bowl, mix avocado with lime juice and stir well.
7. Add this to the quinoa salad and chicken.
8. Toss, coat, and serve.

Nutrition: Calories: 2360; Fat: 120,6 g; Carbs: 229,7 g; Protein: 88,7 g, Cholesterol: 0 mg

CHIPOTLE LIME AVOCADO SALAD

Prep
15 minutes

Cooking Time
0 minutes

Serving
4

Ingredients:

- ¼ cup lime juice
- ¼ cup maple syrup
- ½ tsp chipotle pepper, ground
- ¼ tsp cayenne pepper
- 2 peeled and sliced medium-ripe avocados
- 2 peeled and sliced ½ a medium cucumber
- 1 tbsp fresh chives, minced
- 2 large tomatoes, peeled and cut into ½-inch-thick slices

Directions:

1. Whisk lime juice, maple syrup, chipotle pepper, and, if preferred, cayenne pepper together in a small bowl until well combined.
2. Combine avocados, cucumber, and chives in a separate bowl.
3. Drizzle dressing over the salad and gently mix to coat. Serve with tomatoes on the side.

Nutrition: Calories: 1400, Protein: 27,3 g, Carbs: 78,5 g, Fat: 108,6 g, Cholesterol: 0 mg

EDAMAME AND AVOCADO DIP

Prep 5 minutes | **Cooking Time** 0 minutes | **Serving** 4

Ingredients:

- 1 small avocado
- 12 ounces cooked edamame beans
- ½ onion, chopped.
- ½ cup low-fat Greek yogurt
- 1 lemon, juiced

Directions:

1. Mash the avocado and edamame beans with a fork until smooth.
2. Stir in the onions, Greek yogurt, and lemon juice.
3. Serve immediately.

Nutrition: Calories: 979, Protein: 55,9 g, Carbs: 46,7 g, Fat: 63,1 g, Cholesterol: 0 mg

HEALTHY CARROT CHIPS

Prep
10 minutes

Cooking
10 minutes

Serving
4

Ingredients:

- 3 cups carrots, sliced into paper-thin rounds
- 2 tbsp olive oil
- 2 tsp ground cumin
- ½ tsp smoked paprika
- A pinch salt

Directions:

1. Preheat your oven to 400°F
2. Slice carrot into paper-thin shaped coins using a peeler
3. Place slices in a bowl and toss with oil and spices
4. Layout the slices onto a parchment paper-lined baking sheet in a single layer
5. Sprinkle salt
6. Transfer to oven and bake for 8-10 minutes
7. Remove and serve
8. Enjoy!

Nutrition: Calories: 235, Fat: 10 g, Carbs: 27,1 g, Protein: 4,6 g, Cholesterol: 0 mg

HOMEMADE GUACAMOLE

Prep
10 minutes

Cooking
0 minutes

Serving
2 cups

Ingredients:

- 1 medium ripe avocado, peeled and cubed
- 1 garlic clove, minced
- ¼ to ½ tsp salt
- 1 small onion, finely chopped
- 1 to 2 tbsp lime juice
- 1 tbsp minced fresh cilantro
- 2 medium tomatoes, seeded and chopped, optional

Directions:

1. Mash avocados with garlic and salt.
2. Stir in the remaining ingredients, adding tomatoes.

Nutrition: Calories: 986, Protein: 15,9 g, Carbs: 16 g, Fat: 95,4 g, Cholesterol: 0 mg

HONEY-LIME BERRY SALAD

Prep 15 minutes | **Cooking** 0 minutes | **Serving** 6

Ingredients:

- 4 cups fresh strawberries, halved
- 2 cups fresh blueberries
- 1 medium Granny Smith apple, cubed
- ⅓ cup lime juice
- ¼ to ⅓ cup honey
- 2 tbsp minced fresh mint

Directions:

1. Combine strawberries, blueberries, and apples in a large mixing dish. Combine the lime juice, honey, and mint in a small mixing bowl.
2. Toss the fruit in the dressing to coat.

Nutrition:

Calories: 658, Protein: 8,4 g, Carbs: 147,7 g, Fat: 3,8 g, Cholesterol: 0 mg

NUTS AND SEEDS TRAIL MIX

Prep
5 minutes

Cooking
0 minutes

Serving
5

Ingredients:

- 1/2 cup salted pumpkin seeds or petites
- 1 cup unbranched almonds
- 1 cup unsalted sunflower kernels
- 1 cup walnut halves
- 1 cup dried apricots
- 1 cup dark chocolate chips

Directions:

1. Place all ingredients in a large bowl; toss to combine.
2. Store in an airtight container.

Nutrition:

Calories: 3730, Protein: 95 g, Carbs: 279,6 g, Fat: 248.8 g, Cholesterol: 0 mg

PITA CHIPS

Prep 10 minutes

Cooking 10 minutes

Serving 4

Ingredients:

- ¼ tsp garlic powder
- 1 tbsp grated Parmesan cheese
- ½ tsp salt
- 1 tbsp olive oil
- 1 tbsp dried Italian mixed herbs
- 1 (6-inch) pita bread (whole wheat)

Directions:

1. Preheat the oven to 350°F. Combine Parmesan, garlic powder, Italian mixed herbs, and salt in a mixing bowl.
2. Cut the pita bread into wedges, add to bowl with the rest of the ingredients, and combine well.
3. Place on a baking sheet lined with parchment paper, and bake for 10 minutes or golden brown. Allow cooling on the rack.

Nutrition: Calories: 354, Protein: 8,4 g, Carbs: 29 g, Fat: 22,3 g, Cholesterol: 9 mg

ROASTED BROCCOLI SALAD

Prep 10 minutes
Cooking 17 minutes
Serving 4

Ingredients:

- 1 pound broccoli
- 3 tbsp olive oil
- 2 cup cherry tomatoes
- 1 ½ tsp honey
- 3 cups whole grain bread, cubed
- 1 tbsp balsamic vinegar
- ½ tsp black pepper
- 2 tsp sea salt, fine
- 2 tbsp grated Parmesan cheese for serving

Directions:

1. Set the oven to 450°F, and then heat a rimmed baking sheet.

2. Drizzle your broccoli with a tablespoon of oil and a pinch of salt and toss to coat. Do the same for the cubed bread.

3. Put the broccoli and the bread on a tray with parchment paper and roast for about 15 minutes and stir halfway through your cooking time.

4. Once the broccoli is cooked and the bread is crispy, remove it from the oven and let it cool.

5. Whisk two tablespoons of oil, vinegar, honey, and salt in a bowl until well combined. Add the cherry tomatoes, the broccoli, and the bread and mix.

6. Serve in a bowl and sprinkle the parmesan on top.

Nutrition: Calories: 1383; Fat: 55,5 g; Carbs: 184,9 g; Protein: 35,9 g, Cholesterol: 18 mg

SWEET AND SPICY BRUSSELS SPROUTS

Prep 5 minutes | **Cooking** 20-30 minutes | **Serving** 4

Ingredients:

- 2 pounds brussels sprouts, trimmed and halved
- ¼ cup low-sodium soy sauce
- ¼ cup chili garlic paste
- 3 tbsp honey
- 2 tsp toasted sesame oil

Directions:

1. Preheat the oven to 400°F.

2. Mix the soy sauce, garlic paste, honey, and sesame oil in a bowl. Add the brussels sprout and combine it.

3. Turn the Brussels sprouts onto a large baking sheet and flip them over so they are cut-side down with the flat part touching the baking sheet. Sprinkle with salt and pepper.

4. Bake for 20-30 minutes until the Brussels sprouts are lightly charred, crisp outside, and toasted on the bottom. The outer leaves will be extra dark, too.

5. Serve immediately.

Nutrition: Calories: 1092; Fat: 55,1 g; Carbs: 95,2 g; Protein: 54 g, Cholesterol: 0 mg

SAUTÉED GARLIC MUSHROOMS

Prep	Cooking	Serving
10 minutes	10 minutes	4

Ingredients:

- 1 tbsp olive oil
- 3 garlic cloves, minced
- 16 ounces fresh brown mushrooms, sliced
- 7 ounces fresh shiitake mushrooms, sliced
- ½ tsp salt
- ½ tsp pepper or more to taste

Directions:

1. Place a nonstick saucepan on medium-high heat
2. Add oil and heat for 2 minutes.
3. Stir in the garlic and sauté for a minute.
4. Add the remaining ingredients and stir until soft and tender, for around 5 minutes.
5. Turn off the heat and let the mushrooms rest while the pan is covered for 5 minutes.
6. Serve and enjoy.

Nutrition: Calories 340 ; Fat: 21,6 g; Carbs: 416,2 g; Protein: 14.3 g, Cholesterol: 0 mg

SMOKY CAULIFLOWER

Prep 10 minutes | **Cooking** 25 minutes | **Serving** 4

Ingredients:

- 1 tbsp olive oil
- 1 large cauliflower head: 1-inch florets: about 9 cups
- ¾ tsp salt
- 1 tsp smoked paprika
- 2 tbsp minced fresh parsley
- 2 garlic cloves, minced

Directions:

1. In a large mixing bowl, place the cauliflower. Combine the oil, paprika, and salt. Drizzle the dressing over the cauliflower and toss to coat. Put on a try with parchment paper.

2. Bake for 10 minutes at 450°F, uncovered. Add the garlic and mix well. Bake for 10-15 minutes, stirring periodically until cauliflower is soft and lightly browned. Serve with a parsley garnish.

Nutrition: Calories: 398, Protein: 20,2 g, Carbs: 28,7 g, Fat: 17,1 g, Cholesterol: 0 mg

SWEET CARROTS

Prep 5 minutes | **Cooking** 5 minutes | **Serving** 4

Ingredients:

- ¼ tsp salt
- ½ cup water
- 1 tsp olive oil
- 2 cup shredded carrots
- Honey to taste
- 1 tbsp chopped fresh parsley,
- 1 tsp lemon juice

Directions:

1. Boil water in a small saucepan. Add the shredded carrots and salt. Cook, after covering it, for approximately 5 minutes or until the water has evaporated. Take the carrots off the heat.

2. In a large mixing bowl, combine the lemon juice, honey, olive oil, and parsley with carrots. Serve right away.

Nutrition: Calories: 237, Protein: 3,2 g, Carbs: 44,9 g, Fat: 5 g, Cholesterol: 0 mg

TOFU WITH BRUSSELS SPROUTS

Prep 10 minutes

Cooking 15 minutes

Serving 4

Ingredients:

- 5 tbsp olive oil
- 8 ounces extra-firm tofu, drained, pressed, and cut into slices
- 2 garlic cloves, chopped
- ⅓ cup pecans, toasted and chopped
- 1 tbsp unsweetened applesauce
- ¼ cup fresh cilantro, chopped
- ½-pound Brussels sprouts, trimmed and cut into wide ribbons
- ¾-pound mixed bell peppers, seeded and sliced

Directions:

1. Heat a ½ tablespoon of the oil in a skillet over medium heat and sauté the tofu for about 6–7 minutes, or until golden brown.
2. Add the garlic and pecans and sauté for about 1 minute.
3. Add the applesauce and cook for about 2 minutes.
4. Stir in the cilantro and remove from the heat.
5. Transfer the tofu onto a plate and set aside

6. Heat the remaining oil in the same skillet over medium-high heat and cook the Brussels sprouts and bell peppers for about 5 minutes.

7. Stir in the tofu and remove from the heat.

8. Serve immediately.

Nutrition: Calories: 1854; Fat: 153,3 g; Carbs: 60,1; Protein: 58,4 g, Cholesterol: 0 mg

TOMATO, BASIL AND CUCUMBER SALAD

Prep 10 minutes | **Cooking** 0 minutes | **Serving** 4

Ingredients:

- 1 large cucumber seeded and sliced.
- 4 medium tomatoes, quartered.
- 1 medium red onion thinly sliced.
- ½ cup chopped fresh basil.
- 2 tbsp vinegar
- ½ tsp Dijon mustard
- 1 tbsp extra-virgin olive oil
- ½ tsp black pepper; freshly ground.

Directions:

1. Mix cucumber, tomatoes, red onion, and basil in a medium bowl.

2. Mix vinegar, mustard, olive oil, and pepper in a small bowl.

3. Pour the dressing over the vegetables and gently stir until well combined—cover and chill for at least 30 minutes before serving.

Nutrition: Calories: 258, Protein: 7,2 g, Carbs: 18,5 g, Fat: 17,5 g, Cholesterol: 0 mg

TURMERIC PEPPERS PLATTER

Prep
10 minutes

Cooking
20 minutes

Serving
4

Ingredients:

- 2 green bell peppers, cut into wedges
- 2 red bell peppers, cut into wedges
- 2 yellow bell peppers, cut into wedges
- 2 tbsp avocado oil
- 2 garlic cloves, minced
- A bunch basil, chopped
- A pinch salt and black pepper
- 2 tbsp balsamic vinegar

Directions:

1. Heat a pan with the oil on medium heat, add the garlic, and cook for 2 minutes.
2. Add the peppers, toss, and cook over medium heat for 18 minutes.
3. Add then the balsamic vinegar, stir, cook for another two minutes, and then remove from the heat
4. Arrange them on a platter, sprinkle the chopped basil on top, and serve them as appetizers.

Nutrition: Calories: 324; Fat: 30,7 g; Carbs: 9,7 g; Protein: 2,1 g, Cholesterol: 0 mg

ZUCCHINI PIZZA BITES

Prep: 5 minutes
Cooking: 5 minutes
Serving: 1

Ingredients:

- 1 tbsp quick tomato sauce
- ½ tbsp garlic paste
- ½ tbsp chopped basil
- 2 tbsp extra-virgin olive oil
- 1 medium diagonally cut zucchini.
- ¼ cup part-skim shredded mozzarella
- 1 tbsp salt and pepper

Directions:

1. In a bowl, mix the tomato sauce with the garlic and the basil
2. Cut zucchini into ¼-inch-thick slices. Season both sides with pepper and salt, and oil.
3. Cook the zucchini for 2 minutes on each side on the broiler or the grill, and Broil for a further minute or two after topping with the cheese and the tomato sauce. (Be careful not to overcook the cheese.)

Nutrition: Calories: 551, Protein: 19,4 g, Carbs: 16,3 g, Fat: 41 g, Cholesterol: 15 mg

CHAPTER 7: SOUP AND STEWS RECIPES

COLLARD GREENS DISH

Prep
10 minutes

Cooking
35 minutes

Serving
4

Ingredients:

- 1 tbsp olive oil
- 1 large onion, chopped
- 2 garlic cloves, minced
- 3 cups chicken broth
- 3 bacon slices
- 1 tsp salt
- 1 red pepper flake
- 1 pound fresh collard greens, cut into 2-inch pieces

Directions:

1. Take a large pan and place it over medium-high heat.
2. Add the bacon and cook for 5 minutes, until crispy. Remove them from the heat and chop them.
3. Add the onion to the same pan and cook for 5 minutes

4. Add garlic and cook for another 5 minutes.

5. Add collard greens and the chopped bacon and keep stir-frying until wilted

6. Add the chicken broth and season with salt and red pepper flakes.

7. Reduce the heat and simmer for 20 minutes

Nutrition: Calories: 264, Fat: 129 g, Carbs: 9,2 g, Protein: 16.3 g, Cholesterol: 120 mg

CAULIFLOWER AND HORSERADISH SOUP

Prep
5 minutes

Cooking
30 minutes

Serving
4

Ingredients:

- 2 medium potatoes, peeled and chopped
- 1 medium cauliflower, florets, and stalk chopped
- 1 medium white onion, peeled and chopped
- 1 tsp minced garlic
- ⅔ tsp salt
- ⅓ tsp ground black pepper
- 4 tsp horseradish sauce
- 1 tsp dried thyme
- 3 cups vegetable broth
- 1 cup coconut milk, unsweetened

Directions:

1. In a pot, cook the onion and garlic on medium heat for about 10 minutes.

2. Then add all the vegetables, the thyme, the milk, and the broth, and bring the mixture to a boil.

3. Once boiling, put the heat on a minimum and simmer for 15-20 minutes until the vegetables fall apart.

4. Add salt and black pepper to taste, then use an immersion blender to puree the soup until it is smooth. Serve right away.

Nutrition: Calories: 1065, Fat: 60,7 g, Carbs: 83,9 g, Protein: 45,6 g, Fiber: 28,4 g, Cholesterol: 0 mg

CHICKPEA GARLIC NOODLE SOUP

Prep 5 minutes

Cooking 15 minutes

Serving 6

Ingredients:

- 1 cup cooked chickpeas
- 8 ounces rotini noodles, whole-wheat
- 4 celery stalks, sliced
- 2 medium white onions, peeled and chopped
- 4 medium carrots, peeled and sliced
- 2 tsp minced garlic cloves
- 8 thyme sprigs
- 1 tsp salt
- ⅓ tsp ground black pepper
- 1 bay leaf
- 2 tbsp olive oil
- 2 quarts vegetable broth
- ¼ cup chopped fresh parsley

Directions:

1. Take a large pot, place it over medium heat, add oil, and add all the vegetables, garlic, thyme, and bay leaf and cook for 5 minutes until vegetables are golden.

2. Then pour in the broth, stir, and bring the mixture to a boil.

3. Add chickpeas and noodles into boiling soup, continue cooking for 8 minutes until noodles are tender, and then season the soup with salt and black pepper.

4. Garnish with parsley and serve straight away

Nutrition: Calories: 1668 Cal Fat: 49,5 g Carbs: 242,6 g Protein: 63,4 g Fiber: 57,8 g, Cholesterol: 0 mg

CREAM OF MUSHROOM SOUP

Prep 5 minutes **Cooking** 15 minutes **Serving** 6

Ingredients:

- 1 medium white onion, peeled and chopped
- 16 ounces button mushrooms, sliced
- 1 ½ tsp minced garlic
- ¼ cup all-purpose flour
- ½ tsp ground black pepper
- 1 tsp dried thyme
- ¼ tsp nutmeg
- ½ tsp salt
- 2 tbsp extra-virgin olive oil
- 1 ½ cups coconut milk, unsweetened

- ♟ 4 cups vegetable broth

Directions:

1. Take a large pot, place it over medium-high heat, add the oil, and when it is hot, add onions and garlic, stir in garlic, and cook for 5 minutes until softened.

2. Add the mushroom and cook for about 5 minutes to let the water in the mushroom evaporate.

3. Then sprinkle flour over vegetables, continue cooking for 1 minute, add remaining ingredients, stir until mixed, and simmer for 5 minutes until thickened.

4. Serve straight away

Nutrition: Calories: 884, Fat: 63,8 g, Carbs: 54,2 g, Protein: 23,2 g, Fiber: 37,7 g, Cholesterol: 0 mg

CURRY LENTIL SOUP

Prep
5 minutes

Cooking
40 minutes

Serving
6

Ingredients:

- 1 cup brown lentils
- 1 medium white onion, peeled and chopped
- 28 ounces diced tomatoes
- 1 ½ tsp minced garlic
- 1 inch ginger, grated
- 3 cup vegetable broth
- ½ tsp salt
- 2 tbsp curry powder
- 1 tsp cumin
- ½ tsp cayenne
- 1 tbsp olive oil
- 1 ½ cup coconut milk, unsweetened
- ¼ cup chopped cilantro

Directions:

1. Take a soup pot, place it over medium-high heat, add oil, and when hot, add onion, stir in garlic and ginger, and cook for 5 minutes until golden brown.

2. Then add all the ingredients except milk and cilantro, stir until mixed, and simmer for 25 minutes until the lentils have cooked.

3. When done, stir in milk, cook for 5 minutes until thoroughly heated, and then garnish the soup with cilantro.

4. Serve straight away

Nutrition: Calories: 713; Fat: 42.6 g, Carbs: 56.9 g, Protein: 25.9 g, Fiber: 23.8 g, Cholesterol: 0 mg

FLAVORS VEGETABLE STEW

Prep 10 minutes   **Cooking** 30 minutes   **Serving** 6

Ingredients:

- ½ cup extra-virgin olive oil
- 1 cup frozen peas
- 1 cup frozen corn
- 2 pounds potatoes, peeled & cubed
- 4 large carrots, peeled & diced
- 1 medium onion, chopped
- ½ cup unsweetened coconut milk
- ½ tsp dried oregano
- 1 tsp garlic powder
- 4 cups vegetable broth

- 1 tsp pepper
- Salt to taste

Directions:

1. Add all the vegetables with olive oil to a large pot and, on medium-high heat, cook for about 10 minutes, until golden, to bring up the flavor.

2. Then pour the water, the milk, the pepper, and the salt and cook on low heat for about 20 minutes, until the potato and the carrots are fully cooked.

3. Once the stew is ready, let it rest for 10 minutes before serving.

Nutrition: Calories: 3990; Fat: 244.3 g; Carbs: 385 g; Protein: 62.7 g, Cholesterol: 0 mg

GREEK LENTIL SOUP

Prep
15 minutes

Cooking
45 minutes

Serving
4

Ingredients:

- 8 ounces brown lentils
- ¼ cup extra-virgin olive oil
- 1 tbsp garlic, minced
- 1 medium onion, minced
- 1 large carrot, chopped
- 1 quart water
- 1 pinch dried oregano
- A pinch crushed and dried rosemary
- 2 bay leaves
- 1 tbsp tomato paste
- 1 tbsp salt and black pepper to taste
- 1 tsp olive oil, or to taste
- 1 tsp red wine vinegar

Directions:

1. Add lentils and enough water to cover them in a large saucepan.
2. Boil and cook the lentils for 10 minutes, then drain.

3. Sauté carrot, onion, and garlic with oil in a saucepan over medium heat for 5 minutes.

4. Stir in the bay leaves, rosemary, oregano, black pepper, salt and tomato paste, 1 quart of water, and lentils.

5. Bring to a boil and cook for 30 minutes, until the lentils and vegetables are cooked.

6. Serve warm.

Nutrition: Calories: 845; Fat: 66.9 g, Saturated Fat: 10.88 g, Carbs: 45.1 g, Fiber: 20.2 g, Sugars: 23 g, Protein: 15.6 g, Cholesterol: 0 mg

HEARTY VEGETABLE STEW

Prep 10 minutes   **Cooking** 25 minutes   **Serving** 4

Ingredients:

- 2 tsp olive oil
- 2 celery stalks, chopped
- ½ sweet onion, peeled and chopped
- 1 tsp minced garlic
- 3 cups low-sodium vegetable broth
- 1 cup chopped tomatoes
- 2 carrots, thinly sliced
- 1 cup cauliflower florets
- 1 cup broccoli florets

- 1 yellow bell pepper, diced
- 1 cup low-sodium canned black beans, rinsed & drained
- A pinch red pepper flakes
- Sea salt, to taste
- Freshly ground black pepper
- 2 tbsp grated low-fat Parmesan cheese for garnish
- 1 tbsp chopped fresh parsley, for garnish

Directions:

1. In a large saucepan, warm the olive oil over medium-high heat.
2. Add celery, onions, garlic, and sauté until softened, about 4 minutes.
3. Stir in the vegetable broth, tomatoes, carrots, cauliflower, broccoli, bell peppers, black beans, and red pepper flakes.
4. Bring the stew to a boil, then reduce the heat to low and simmer until the vegetables are tender, 18 to 20 minutes.
5. Season with salt and pepper.
6. Serve topped with Parmesan cheese and parsley.

Nutrition: Calories: 834; Fat: 39.4 g; Carbs: 84.4 g; Protein: 35.8 g, Cholesterol: 0 mg

INDIAN VEGETABLE STEW

Prep
10 minutes

Cooking
70 minutes

Serving
4

Ingredients:

- 4 tbsp vegetable oil
- 1 (15-oz/425-g) can chickpeas, drained & rinsed
- 4 cup water
- 1 (15-ounce/425-g) can no-salt-added diced tomatoes
- 2 medium sweet potatoes, peeled and diced
- 1 medium onion, diced
- 1 bell pepper, seeded and diced
- 2 garlic cloves, minced
- 1 tbsp curry powder
- 1 ½ tsp ground ginger
- ½ tsp salt
- 1 tsp ground cumin
- 1 tsp ground turmeric
- 1 tsp ground coriander

- 1 tsp red pepper flakes
- ½ pint cherry tomatoes halved
- ½ cup frozen peas
- Chopped fresh parsley for garnish (optional)

Directions:

1. In a pot on medium heat, cook the onion, the garlic, and the ginger for about 5 minutes.
2. Add then the spices and stir for another 5 minutes.
3. Once the mix begins to brown, add the chickpeas, water, sweet potatoes, and bell pepper. Stir to mix well.
4. Cook on low for 30 minutes.
5. After 30 minutes, stir in the cherry tomatoes and peas. Mix well and cook for the remaining 30 minutes.
6. Garnish with parsley (if using) and serve.

Nutrition: Calories: 1480; Fat: 73.7 g; Carbs: 154.7 g; Protein: 50.1 g, Cholesterol: 0 mg

LENTIL VEGGIE STEW

Prep 10 minutes
Cooking 2 hours
Serving 4

Ingredients:

- 1 cup green lentils, rinsed
- ¼ cup olive oil
- ¼ tsp chili powder
- ½ tsp dried thyme
- ½ tsp dried oregano
- ½ cup wheat berries
- 4 cups vegetable broth
- 1 tsp garlic cloves, minced
- 2 potatoes, peeled & diced
- 3 carrots, peeled & diced
- 2 celery stalks, sliced
- 1 medium onion, chopped
- Pepper
- Salt

Directions:

1. Add green lentils and remaining ingredients into the slow cooker and stir well.

2. Cover and then cook on high for 2 hours.

3. Stir well and serve.

Nutrition: Calories: 1362; Fat: 64.2 g; Carbs: 141.2 g; Protein: 54.5 g, Cholesterol: 0 m

MEXICAN LENTIL SOUP

Prep 5 minutes | **Cooking** 45 minutes | **Serving** 6

Ingredients:

- 2 cup green lentils
- 1 medium red bell pepper, cored, diced
- 1 medium white onion, peeled, diced
- 2 cup diced tomatoes
- 8 ounces diced green chilies
- 2 celery stalks, diced
- 2 medium carrots, peeled, diced
- 1 ½ tsp minced garlic
- ½ tsp salt
- 1 tbsp cumin
- ¼ tsp smoked paprika
- 1 tsp oregano

- ⅛ tsp hot sauce

- 2 tbsp olive oil

- 8 cups vegetable broth

- ¼ cup cilantro, for garnish

- 1 avocado, peeled, pitted, diced, for garnish

Directions:

1. Take a large pot over medium heat, add oil, and when hot, add all the vegetables, reserving tomatoes and chilies, and cook for 5 minutes until softened.

2. Then add garlic, stir in oregano, cumin, and paprika, and continue cooking for 1 minute.

3. Add lentils, tomatoes, and green chilies, season with salt, pour in the broth and simmer the soup for 40 minutes until cooked.

4. When done, ladle soup into bowls, top with avocado and cilantro, and serve straight away

Nutrition: Calories: 1538, Fat: 94.6 g, Carbs: 116 g, Protein: 55.8 g, Fiber: 53.7 g, Cholesterol: 0 mg

PORTOBELLO MUSHROOM STEW

Prep	Cooking	Serving
10 minutes	30 minutes	4

Ingredients:

- 2 tbsp extra-virgin olive oil

- 8 cups vegetable broth

- 1 cup dried wild mushrooms

- 1 cup dried chickpeas
- 3 cups chopped potato
- 2 cups chopped carrots
- 1 cup corn kernels
- 2 cups diced white onions
- 1 tbsp minced parsley
- 3 cups chopped zucchini
- 1 tbsp minced rosemary
- 1 ½ tsp ground black pepper
- 1 tsp dried sage
- ⅔ tsp salt
- 1 tsp dried oregano
- 3 tbsp soy sauce
- 1 ½ tsp liquid smoke
- 8 ounces tomato paste

Directions:

1. Heat the olive oil in a large pot on medium heat and stir in the vegetables. Cook for about 10 minutes.

2. Add then all the rest of the ingredients and bring to a boil.

3. Put on low heat and cook for about 20 minutes until the vegetables are fully cooked, and the stew thickens.

Nutrition: Calories: 2470, Fat: 63.1 g, Carbs: 366.8 g, Protein: 109.1 g, Fiber: 188 g, Cholesterol: 0 mg

ROOT VEGETABLE STEW

Prep
10 minutes

Cooking
70 minutes

Serving
6

Ingredients:

- 2 cups chopped kale
- 1 large white onion, peeled and chopped
- 1 pound parsnips, peeled and chopped
- 1 pound potatoes, peeled and chopped
- 2 celery ribs, chopped
- 1 pound butternut squash, peeled, deseeded, and chopped
- 1 pound carrots, peeled and chopped
- 3 tsp minced garlic
- 1 pound sweet potatoes, peeled and chopped
- 1 bay leaf
- 1 tsp ground black pepper
- ½ tsp sea salt
- 1 tbsp chopped sage
- 3 cups vegetable broth

Directions:

1. Switch on the slow cooker, add all the ingredients except for the kale, and stir until mixed.
2. Shut the cooker with the lid and cook for 1 hour at a low heat setting until cooked.
3. When done, add kale to the stew, stir until mixed, and cook for 10 minutes until leaves have wilted.
4. Serve straight away.

Nutrition: Calories: 1558, Fat: 12.2 g, Carbs: 317.3 g, Protein: 45.3 g, Fiber: 59.2 g, Cholesterol: 0 mg

SAVORY CHICKEN AND WATERMELON RIND SOUP

Prep
10 minutes

Cooking
35 minutes

Serving
4

Ingredients:

- 1 tbsp olive oil
- ¾ pound (340 g) boneless, skinless chicken thighs
- 2 tbsp minced garlic
- 1 tsp peeled minced fresh ginger
- A pinch sea salt
- A pinch freshly ground black pepper
- 6 cups water
- 3 cups diced watermelon rind

Directions:

1. In a huge stockpot, heat the olive oil over medium heat. Add the chicken, garlic, ginger, salt, pepper, and sauté until the chicken is no longer pink for about 5 minutes.

2. Add the water to the pot, increase the heat to high, and bring the soup to a boil.

3. Add the watermelon rind once the water comes to a boil.

4. Let the soup boil again, reduce the heat to medium, and simmer for 30 minutes.

5. Add more salt, if desired, and enjoy immediately.

Nutrition: Calories: 793; Fat: 35.9 g; Carbs: 50.7 g; Protein: 66.7 g, Cholesterol: 299.2 mg

SPICY LENTIL CHILI

Prep 10 minutes **Cooking** 20 minutes **Serving** 4

Ingredients:

- 1 tbsp olive oil
- 1 onion, chopped
- 5 garlic cloves, minced
- 1 Jalapeño pepper, seeded and minced
- 1 cup red lentils, sorted and rinsed
- 1 tbsp chili powder
- 1 tsp smoked paprika
- ⅛ tsp red pepper flakes
- 1 (14-ounce/397-g) can no-salt-added diced tomatoes, undrained

- 3 tbsp no-salt-added tomato paste
- 1 (16-ounce/454-g) can of low-sodium kidney beans, rinsed and drained
- ⅓ cup chopped fresh cilantro leaves

Directions:

1. In a large saucepan, heat the olive oil over medium heat.
2. Add the onion, garlic, and jalapeño pepper, and cook and stir for 2 minutes.
3. Add the lentils, chili powder, paprika, red pepper flakes, tomatoes, tomato paste, and kidney beans, and bring to a boil.
4. Lower the heat, partially cover the pan, and simmer for 15 to 18 minutes until the chili powder has blended in and the lentils are tender. Top with fresh cilantro and serve.

Nutrition: Calories: 714; Fat: 20.5 g; Carbs: 97.6 g; Protein: 34.5 g, Cholesterol: 0 mg

THICK & CREAMY POTATO SOUP

Prep	Cooking	Serving
10 minutes	60 minutes	6

Ingredients:

- 6 cups sweet potatoes, diced
- ¼ tsp cinnamon
- ¼ tsp nutmeg
- ½ cup peanut butter, creamy
- 4 cups vegetable broth

- 🧑‍🍳 1 tbsp ginger garlic paste
- 🧑‍🍳 1 onion, diced
- 🧑‍🍳 Pepper
- 🧑‍🍳 Salt

Directions:

1. Add all the ingredients into the slow cooker and stir well.
2. Cover and cook on low for 1 hour
3. Puree the soup using a blender until smooth.
4. Stir well and serve.

Nutrition: Calories: 2015; Fat: 77.4 g; Carbs: 282.3 g; Protein: 47.5 g, Cholesterol: 0 mg

TUSCAN FISH STEW

Prep 10 minutes | **Cooking** 20 minutes | **Serving** 4

Ingredients:

- 🧑‍🍳 1 tbsp olive oil
- 🧑‍🍳 1 onion, chopped
- 🧑‍🍳 2 garlic cloves, minced
- 🧑‍🍳 3 large tomatoes, chopped
- 🧑‍🍳 1 bulb fennel, peeled, chopped, and rinsed

- 1 (14-ounce/397-g) can of artichoke hearts, drained
- 1 bay leaf
- ⅛ tsp red pepper flakes
- 2 cups low-sodium vegetable broth
- ¾ pound (340 g) halibut fillets, cubed
- ¼ pound (113 g) of sea scallops
- 1 slice low-sodium whole-wheat bread, crumbled
- 2 tbsp chopped fresh basil
- 2 tsp chopped fresh oregano
- 2 tbsp chopped fresh flat-leaf parsley

Directions:

1. Heat the olive oil over medium heat in a stockpot.
2. Add the onion and garlic, and then cook while stirring for 3 minutes.
3. Add the tomatoes, fennel, artichoke hearts, bay leaf, red pepper flakes, and vegetable broth, and bring to a simmer. Simmer for 5 minutes.
4. Add the halibut fillets, and simmer for 4 minutes. Then add the scallops, and simmer for 3 minutes, or until the fillets flake when tested with a fork and the scallops are opaque.
5. Stir in the bread crumbs, then cover the pan and remove from the heat. Let it stand for 3 minutes.
6. Remove and discard the bay leaf. Top the soup with fresh basil, oregano, and parsley, and serve.

Nutrition: Calories: 1218; Fat: 68.2 g; Carbs: 62.5 g; Protein: 88.7 g, Cholesterol: 216.8 mg

CHAPTER 8: POULTRY RECIPES

ASIAN CHICKEN BREASTS

Prep 8 hours | **Cooking** 10 minutes | **Serving** 4

Ingredients:

- 1 pound chicken breasts, boneless & skinless
- 1 ½ tbsp fish sauce
- ½ cup unsweetened coconut milk
- 1 ½ tbsp red curry paste
- 1 tsp brown sugar
- Pepper
- Salt

Directions:

1. Add chicken and remaining ingredients into the zip-lock bag.
2. Seal the bag and place it in the refrigerator for 8 hours.
3. Place marinated chicken on a hot grill and cook for 10 minutes. Turn halfway through.
4. Serve and enjoy.

Nutrition: Calories: 796; Fat: 37.5 g; Carbs: 24.3 g; Protein: 90.3 g, Cholesterol: 400 mg

CHICKEN THIGHS AND APPLES MIX

Prep: 10 minutes
Cooking: 60 minutes
Serving: 4

Ingredients:

- 3 cored and sliced apples
- 1 tbsp apple cider vinegar treatment
- ¾ cup natural apple juice
- ¼ tsp pepper and salt
- 1 tbsp grated ginger
- 8 chicken thighs
- 3 tbsp chopped onion

Directions:

1. Mix chicken with salt, pepper, vinegar, onion, ginger, and apple juice in a bowl, toss well, cover, and keep in the fridge for at least 1 hour.

2. Transfer to a tray with parchment paper, and include apples. Put inside the oven at 400°F for 1 hour. Divide between plates and serve.

Nutrition: Calories: 2516, Carbs: 85.8 g, Fat: 76.1 g, Protein: 371.9 g, Cholesterol: 408 mg

CHICKEN TIKKA

Prep
2-4 hours

Cooking
20 minutes

Serving
6

Ingredients:

- 4 chicken breasts, skinless, boneless; cubed
- 2 large onions, cut into chunks
- 10 cherry tomatoes
- ⅓ cup plain non-fat yogurt
- 4 garlic cloves, crushed
- 1 ½ fresh ginger, peeled and chopped
- 1 small onion, grated
- 1 ½ tsp chili powder
- 1 tbsp ground coriander
- 1 tsp salt
- 2 tbsp coriander leaves

Directions:

1. Combine the non-fat yogurt, grated onion, crushed garlic, ginger, chili powder, coriander, salt, and pepper in a large bowl. Add the cubed chicken and stir until the chicken is coated.

2. Cover with plastic film and place in the fridge. Marinate for 2 – 4 hours.

3. Heat the broiler or barbecue.

4. After marinating the chicken, prepare some skewers—alternate chicken pieces, cherry tomatoes, and onion chunks onto the skewers.

5. Grill for 6 – 8 minutes on each side. Once the chicken is cooked, pull the meat and vegetables off the skewers and put them onto plates. Garnish with coriander. Serve immediately.

Nutrition: Calories: 913; Fat: 7.2 g; Carbs: 38.1 g; Protein: 174.1 g, Cholesterol: 509 mg

CHICKEN TORTILLAS

Prep 10 minutes

Cooking 5 minutes

Serving 4

Ingredients:

- 6 ounces boneless, skinless, and cooked chicken breasts
- Black pepper and salt to taste
- 1 tsp minced garlic cloves
- ⅓ cup fat-free yogurt
- 4 heated-up whole-wheat tortillas
- 2 chopped tomatoes

Directions:

1. In a bowl, mix the yogurt, garlic, salt, and pepper and combine them.

2. Heat a pan over medium heat, and cook both sides of the tortillas. Once slightly browned, remove from the heat and put on a plate.

3. Spread the yogurt dressing on each tortilla, add chicken and tomatoes, roll, and serve.

Nutrition: Calories:1560, Carbs: 176.6 g, Fat: 55.9 g, Protein: 87.7 g, Potassium 1244 mg, Cholesterol: 149.7 mg

CLASSIC CHICKEN COOKING WITH TOMATOES & TAPENADE

Prep 10 minutes **Cooking** 25 minutes **Serving** 4

Ingredients:

- 4–5 ounces chicken breasts, boneless and skinless
- 1 tbsp olive oil
- ¼ tsp salt
- 3 tbsp fresh basil leaves, chopped
- 1 ½ cup cherry tomatoes halved
- ¼ cup olive tapenade

Directions:

1. Arrange the chicken on a sheet of glassine or waxed paper. Sprinkle half of the salt over the chicken. Then flip it and put the rest of the salt. Cover it with another sheet of waxed paper.

2. Flatten the chicken to a half-inch thickness using a meat mallet or rolling pin.

3. Heat the olive oil in a non-stick pan placed over medium-high heat. Once it is hot, add the chicken

4. Cook for 6 minutes on each side until it turns golden brown and fully cooked. Transfer the browned chicken breasts to a platter, and cover them to keep them warm.

5. In the same pan, add the olive tapenade and tomatoes. Cook for 3 minutes until the tomatoes begin to be tender. Remove from the heat, add half of the fresh basil, and mix well.

6. To serve, pour the tomato-tapenade mixture over the cooked chicken breasts and top with the remaining basil.

Nutrition: Calories: 437, Carbs: 7 g, Fat: 29.2 g, Fiber: 5.5 g, Protein: 36.2 g, Potassium 608 mg, Cholesterol: 124.7 mg

DELICIOUS CHICKEN TENDERS

Prep	Cooking	Serving
6 hours	10 minutes	4

Ingredients:

- 1 ½ pounds chicken tenders
- 1 ½ tbsp fresh rosemary, chopped
- 3 tbsp maple syrup
- ¼ cup Dijon mustard
- 2 tbsp olive oil
- 1 tbsp lemon juice
- Pepper
- Salt

Directions:

1. Add chicken tenders and remaining ingredients into the zip-lock bag.
2. Seal the bag and place it in the refrigerator for 6 hours.
3. Place marinated chicken tenders on a hot grill and cook for 10 minutes. Turn halfway through.
4. Serve and enjoy.

Nutrition: Calories: 2092; Fat: 86.1 g; Carbs: 36.3 g; Protein: 293.2 g, Cholesterol: 598.7 mg

GARLIC MUSHROOM CHICKEN

Prep 10 minutes | **Cooking** 10 minutes | **Serving** 4

Ingredients:

- 4 chicken breasts, boneless and skinless
- 3 garlic cloves, minced
- 1 onion, chopped
- 2 cups mushrooms, sliced
- 1 tbsp olive oil
- ½ cup chicken stock
- ¼ tsp pepper
- ½ tsp salt

Directions:

1. Season chicken with pepper and salt. Warm oil in a pan on medium heat, then put seasoned chicken in the pan and cook for 5 minutes on each side. Remove and place on a plate.

2. Add onion and mushrooms to the pan and sauté until tender, about 2–3 minutes. Add garlic and sauté for a minute. Add stock and the chicken and bring to a boil. Stir well and cook for 10 minutes.

3. Serve.

Nutrition: Calories: 1614, Carbs: 12 g, Fat: 16.6 g, Protein: 353.9 g, Sodium 1429 mg, Potassium 6881 mg, Cholesterol: 598.8 mg

GRILLED CHICKEN

Prep
60 minutes

Cooking
10 minutes

Serving
4

Ingredients:

- 4 chicken breasts, skinless and boneless
- 1 ½ tsp dried oregano
- 1 tsp paprika
- 5 garlic cloves, minced
- ½ cup fresh parsley, minced
- ½ cup olive oil
- ½ cup fresh lemon juice
- Pepper

- 🎩 Salt

Directions:

1. Add lemon juice, oregano, paprika, garlic, parsley, and olive oil to a large zip-lock bag. Season chicken with pepper and salt and add to bag. Seal the bag and shake well to coat the chicken with marinade. Let sit chicken in the marinade for 60 minutes.

2. Remove chicken from the marinade and grill over medium-high heat for 5-6 minutes on each side. Serve and enjoy.

Nutrition: Calories: 2364, Fat: 112.9 g, Protein: 328.4 g, Carbs: 8.4 g, Sodium: 468 mg, Sodium: 468 mg, Cholesterol: 598.8 mg

HEALTHY CHICKEN ORZO

Prep 10 minutes | **Cooking** 15 minutes | **Serving** 4

Ingredients:

- 🎩 1 cup whole wheat orzo
- 🎩 1 pound chicken breasts, sliced
- 🎩 ½ tsp red pepper flakes
- 🎩 ½ cup feta cheese, crumbled
- 🎩 ½ tsp oregano
- 🎩 1 tbsp fresh parsley, chopped
- 🎩 1 tbsp fresh basil, chopped
- 🎩 ¼ cup pine nuts

- 1 cup spinach, chopped
- ¼ cup white wine
- ½ cup olives, sliced
- 1 cup grape tomatoes, cut in half
- ½ tbsp garlic, minced
- 2 tbsp olive oil
- ½ tsp pepper
- ½ tsp salt

Directions:

1. Add water to a small saucepan and bring to a boil.
2. Heat 1 tbsp olive oil in a pan over medium heat. Season chicken with pepper and salt and cook in the pan for 5–7 minutes on each side. Remove from pan and set aside.
3. Add orzo to boiling water and cook according to the packet directions. Heat the remaining olive oil in a pan on medium heat, then put garlic in the pan and sauté for a minute. Stir in white wine and cherry tomatoes and cook on high for 3 minutes.
4. Add cooked orzo, spices, spinach, pine nuts, and olives and stir until well combined. Add chicken on top of the orzo and sprinkle with feta cheese. Serve and enjoy.

Nutrition: Calories: 2007, Carbs: 132 g, Fat: 89.9 g, Protein: 159.6 g, Sodium 1656 mg, Cholesterol: 399.2 mg

HOT CHICKEN WINGS

Prep	Cooking	Serving
10 minutes	20 minutes	4

Ingredients:

- 10 - 20 chicken wings
- 1 bottle Durkee hot sauce
- 2 tbsp honey
- 10 shakes Tabasco sauce
- 2 tbsp cayenne pepper

Directions:

1. Heat the oven to 350°F, place the chicken wings on a tray with parchment paper, and cook for approximately 20 minutes, until the chicken is fully cooked.
2. Mix the hot sauce, honey, Tabasco, and cayenne pepper in a medium bowl. Mix well.
3. Mix the chicken wings in the sauce until coated evenly.
4. Serve hot.

Nutrition: Calories: 3354; Fat: 175.9 g; Carbs: 87.7 g; Protein: 355.3 g, Cholesterol: 460 mg

JUICY CHICKEN PATTIES

Prep
10 minutes

Cooking
10 minutes

Serving
4

Ingredients:

- 1 pound ground chicken
- 2 tbsp olive oil
- ¼ tsp red pepper flakes
- 1 scallion, chopped
- 1 egg yolk
- Pepper
- Salt

Directions:

1. Mix chicken, red pepper flakes, scallions, egg yolk, pepper, and salt until well combined in a mixing bowl.
2. Heat oil in a pan over medium-high heat.
3. Make small patties from the chicken mixture.
4. Place patties in hot oil and cook for 2-3 minutes on each side.
5. Serve and enjoy.

Nutrition: Calories: 918; Fat: 56.8 g; Carbs: 24.7 g; Protein: 77 g, Cholesterol: 1484.2 mg

SPICY CHICKEN

Prep
6 hours

Cooking
20 minutes

Serving
2

Ingredients:

- 2 chicken breasts, boneless
- 1 ½ tsp chili powder
- 3 tbsp sriracha sauce
- ¼ tsp smoked paprika
- 2 tbsp sesame oil
- 1 tbsp brown sugar
- 1 tsp onion powder
- 1 tsp garlic powder
- Salt

Directions:

1. Add all the ingredients to a bowl and mix until well-coated.
2. Cover the bowl and place it in the refrigerator for 6 hours.
3. Preheat the oven to 350°F. Place the marinated chicken on parchment paper tray, and cook for about 20 minutes. Turn halfway through.
4. Serve and enjoy.

Nutrition: Calories: 948; Fat: 7 g; Carbs: 21.7 g; Protein: 199.7 g, Cholesterol: 299.4 mg

TASTY CHICKEN WINGS

Prep 10 minutes | **Cooking** 12 minutes | **Serving** 4

Ingredients:

- 15 chicken wings
- ½ tsp coriander
- ½ tsp cumin powder
- ¼ tsp ground ginger
- ½ tsp turmeric
- 1 tbsp dried rosemary
- 1 ½ tsp smoked paprika
- 1 ½ tsp garlic powder
- 1 ½ tsp onion powder
- Pepper
- Salt

Directions:

1. Add chicken wings into the large mixing bowl.
2. Add remaining ingredients over chicken wings and mix until well coated.
3. Place chicken wings on preheated grill and cook for 8-12 minutes or until cooked.
4. Serve and enjoy.

Nutrition: Calories: 3934; Fat: 250.9 g; Carbs: 9.6 g; Protein: 409.3 g, Cholesterol: 355 mg

CHAPTER 9: PORK AND MEAT RECIPES

BEEF VEGGIE POT MEAL

Prep
20 minutes

Cooking
40 minutes

Serving
4

Ingredients:

- 1 tsp extra-virgin olive oil
- ½ cup water
- ¼ shredded cabbage head
- 2 peeled and sliced carrots
- 1 tbsp flour & 4 tbsp sour cream
- 1 chopped onion
- 10 ounces sliced and boiled beef tenderloin

Directions:

1. Add the oil, cabbage, carrots, and onions in a saucepan.
2. Cook on medium-high heat until the veggies get softened.
3. Add the beef meat and stir the mix. Let it brown.
4. Mix the cream with flour and the water until smooth in a mixing bowl.

5. Add the sauce over the beef.

6. Cover and cook for 40 minutes. Serve warm.

Nutrition: Calories: 802, Fat: 45.1 g, Carbs: 34.5 g, Protein: 64.3 g, Sodium: 417 mg, Cholesterol: 286.3 mg

BEEF WITH MUSHROOMS

Prep 10 minutes | **Cooking** 4 hours | **Serving** 4

Ingredients:

- 2 cups salt-free tomato paste
- 2 cups sliced fresh mushrooms
- 2 cups low-fat, low-sodium: beef broth
- 2 pounds cubed lean beef stew meat
- 1 cup chopped fresh parsley leaves
- Freshly ground black pepper
- 4 minced garlic cloves

Directions:

1. Add all ingredients except lemon juice and stir to combine in a slow cooker.

2. Set the slow cooker on low.

3. Cover and cook for about 4 hours.

4. Serve hot with the drizzling of lemon juice.

Nutrition: Calories: 1616, Fat: 35.6 g, Carbs: 100.1 g, Protein: 223.6 g, Sodium: 2540 mg, Potassium: 6736 mg, Cholesterol: 726.2 mg

BRAISED BEEF SHANKS

Prep 10 minutes | **Cooking** 80 minutes | **Serving** 4

Ingredients:

- Freshly ground black pepper to taste
- 5 minced garlic cloves
- 1 tbsp extra-virgin olive oil
- 1 ½ pounds lean beef shanks
- 2 sprigs fresh rosemary
- 1 cup low-fat, low-sodium: beef broth
- 1 tbsp fresh lime juice

Directions:

1. In a big pot, heat the oil on medium heat; once it is hot, add the meat and let it caramelize for about 5 minutes.
2. Once it is browned, add the rest of the ingredients and mix well.
3. Set the heat low, cover, and cook for about 1 hour.
4. Let the stew rest for about 20 minutes before serving it.

Nutrition: Calories: 2211, Fat: 95.1 g, Carbs: 8.6 g, Protein: 330.4 g, Sodium: 1416 mg, Potassium: 5405 mg, Cholesterol: 530.7 mg

CITRUS PORK

Prep 10 minutes | **Cooking** 30 minutes | **Serving** 4

Ingredients:

- 2 limes zest, grated
- 1 orange zest, grated
- 1 orange, juiced
- 2 limes, juiced
- 4 tsp garlic cloves, minced
- 1/4 cup olive oil
- 1 cup cilantro, chopped
- 1 cup mint, chopped
- Black pepper to the taste
- 4 pork loin steaks

Directions:

1. Mix lime zest and Juice with orange zest and juice, garlic, oil, cilantro, mint, and pepper in your food processor.

2. Put the steaks in a bowl, add the citrus mix, and toss well.

3. Heat a pan over medium-high heat, add pork steaks and the marinade, cook for 4 minutes on each side, introduce the pan to the oven, and bake at 350°F for 20 minutes.

4. Divide the steaks between plates, drizzle some cooking juices, and serve with a side salad.

Nutrition: Calories: 1693, Fat: 106.7 g, Fiber: 12 g, Carbs: 29.9 g, Protein: 153.4 g, Sodium: 17 mg, Potassium: 617 mg, Cholesterol: 640 mg

EASY VEAL CHOPS

Prep 10 minutes **Cooking** 20 minutes **Serving** 4

Ingredients:

- 3 tbsp whole wheat flour
- Black pepper and salt to the taste
- 2 eggs
- 1 tbsp milk
- 1 ½ cup whole-wheat breadcrumbs
- 1 lemon zest, grated
- 4 veal rib chops

Directions:

1. Put whole wheat flour in a bowl.
2. In another bowl, mix eggs with milk and whisk
3. In a third bowl, mix the breadcrumbs with lemon zest.

4. Season veal chops with black pepper and salt, dredge them in flour, dip in the egg mix, and then in breadcrumbs. Repeat this process twice

5. Heat the oven to 350°F. Transfer the veal ribs to a baking sheet, put them in the oven, and bake for 20 minutes until fully cooked inside and crispy outside.

6. Divide between plates and serve with a side salad.

Nutrition: Calories: 1664, Fat: 71 g, Fiber: 4.3 g, Carbs: 26.3 g, Protein: 230.1 g, Sodium: 560 mg, Potassium: 3439 mg, Cholesterol: 828mg

GARLIC LIME MARINATED PORK CHOPS

Prep 20 minutes | **Cooking** 20 minutes | **Serving** 4

Ingredients:

- 4 (6 ounces each) lean boneless pork chops
- 4 garlic cloves, crushed
- 1 tsp cumin
- 1 tsp chili powder
- 1 tsp paprika
- Fresh black pepper to taste
- ½ lime (about 1 tbsp), juiced
- ½ lime, zest

Directions:

1. Season the pork with all the spices, lime juice, zest, and garlic in a bowl.

2. Marinate for 20 minutes.

3. Layer the broiler pan with tin foil.

4. Place the seasoned pork in the pan and broil for 10 minutes per side until fully cooked.

5. Serve warm.

Nutrition: Calories 781, Sodium: 488 mg, Potassium: 2572 mg, Carbs: 8.6 g, Fiber: 2.9 g, Protein: 140.8 g, Cholesterol: 530.8 mg

GRILLED FENNEL-CUMIN LAMB CHOPS

Prep
30 minutes

Cooking
15 minutes

Serving
4

Ingredients:

- ¼ tsp salt
- 1 minced large garlic clove
- ⅛ tsp cracked black pepper
- ¾ tsp crushed fennel seeds
- ¼ tsp ground coriander
- 4-6 sliced lamb rib chops
- ¾ tsp ground cumin

Directions:

1. Trim fat from chops. Place the chops on a plate.

2. In a small bowl, combine garlic, fennel seeds, cumin, salt, coriander, and black pepper. Sprinkle the mixture evenly over the chops; rub it with your fingers. Cover the chops with plastic wrap and marinate in the refrigerator for at least 30 minutes or up to 24 hours.

3. Grill the lamb for about 15 minutes or until it reaches the desired cooking point.

Nutrition: Calories: 934, Fat: 25.2 g, Carbs: 9.5 g, Protein: 167.1 g, Sugar: 9.5 g, Sodium: 589 mg, Potassium 3018 mg, Cholesterol: 598.8 mg

HEALTHY BEEF CABBAGE

Prep 10 minutes | **Cooking** 10 minutes | **Serving** 4

Ingredients:

- 4 tbsp sour cream
- ¼ shredded cabbage head
- 1 tsp butter
- 2 peeled and sliced carrots
- 1 chopped onion
- 10 ounces boiled and sliced beef tenderloin
- 1 tbsp flour

Directions:

1. Sauté the cabbage, carrots, and onions in butter.
2. Spray a pot with cooking spray.

3. In layers, place the sautéed vegetables, then beef, then another layer of vegetables.

4. Mix the sour cream with flour until smooth and pour over the pot on the layers of vegetables and beef.

5. Cover and bake at 400°F for 40 minutes.

Nutrition: Calories: 701, Fat: 27.4 g, Carbs: 43.5 g, Protein: 69.9 g, Sugar: 28.5 g, Sodium: 379 mg, Potassium: 1949 mg, Cholesterol: 241 mg

HEALTHY MEATBALLS

Prep	Cooking	Serving
10 minutes	20 minutes	6

Ingredients:

- 2 eggs
- 2 pounds ground chicken
- 1 ½ tbsp garlic cloves, minced
- 1 small onion, chopped
- ½ cup cilantro, chopped
- 8 ounces goat cheese, crumbled
- 20 ounces kale, frozen, thawed & squeezed
- ½ cup almond flour
- Pepper to taste
- Salt to taste

Directions:

1. Preheat the oven to 400°F.
2. Add chicken and remaining ingredients into the large mixing bowl and mix until well combined.
3. Make a similar shape of balls from the chicken mixture and place them onto a parchment-lined baking sheet.
4. Bake in preheated oven for 15-20 minutes.
5. Serve and enjoy.

Nutrition: Calories: 1969; Fat: 109.1 g; Carbs: 48.7 g; Protein: 198.1 g Cholesterol: 1170 mg

HEARTY PORK BELLY CASSEROLE

Prep 10 minutes | **Cooking** 45 minutes | **Serving** 4

Ingredients:

- 8 pork belly slices, cut into small pieces
- 3 large onions, chopped
- 4 tbsp honey
- 1 lemon, zest
- Salt to taste

Directions:

1. Take a large pressure cooker and place it over medium heat.

2. Add onions and sweat them for 5 minutes.

3. Add pork belly slices and cook until the meat browns and the onions become golden.

4. Cover with water, add honey, lemon zest, and pepper, and close the pressure seal.

5. Pressure cooks for 40 minutes.

6. Serve and enjoy with a garnish of fresh chopped parsley, if you prefer.

Nutrition: Calories: 2893, Fat: 128.5 g, Carbs: 89 g, Protein: 345.3 g, Sodium: 46 mg, Potassium: 579 mg, Cholesterol: 576.3 mg

JERK BEEF AND PLANTAIN KABOBS

Prep	Cooking	Serving
10 minutes	15 minutes	4

Ingredients:

- 2 peeled and sliced ripe plantains
- 2 tbsp red wine vinegar
- Lime wedges & 1 tbsp cooking oil
- 1 sliced medium red onion
- 12 ounces sliced boneless beef sirloin steak
- 1 tbsp Jamaican jerk seasoning

Directions:

1. Trim fat from meat. Cut into 1-inch pieces. In a small bowl, stir together red wine vinegar, oil, and jerk seasoning.

2. Toss meat cubes with half of the vinegar mixture. On long skewers, alternately thread meat, plantain chunks, and onion wedges, leaving a ¼-inch space between pieces.

3. Brush plantains and onion wedges with the remaining vinegar mixture.

4. Place skewers on the rack of an uncovered grill directly over medium coals.

5. Grill for 12 to 15 minutes or until meat is the desired doneness, turning occasionally.

6. Serve with lime wedges.

Nutrition: Calories: 1000, Fat: 43.2 g, Carbs: 76.5 g, Protein: 76.6 g, Sugar: 39.1 g, Sodium: 16 mg, Potassium: 181 mg, Cholesterol: 313 mg

LAMB CHOPS WITH ROSEMARY

Prep 10 minutes | **Cooking** 15 minutes | **Serving** 4

Ingredients:

- 1 pound lamb chops
- ½ tsp freshly ground black pepper
- 1 tbsp olive oil
- 5 garlic cloves
- 1 tbsp chopped fresh rosemary

Directions:

1. Adjust the oven rack to the top third of the oven. Preheat broiler. Line a baking sheet with foil. Place the garlic, rosemary, pepper, and olive oil into a small bowl and stir well to combine.

2. Place the lamb chops on a baking sheet and brush half of the garlic-rosemary mixture equally between the chops, coating well. Place the sheet beneath the broiler and broil for 4–5 minutes.

3. Remove from the oven and carefully flip over the chops. Divide the remaining garlic-rosemary mixture evenly between the chops and spread to coat. Return pan to oven and broil for another 3 minutes. Remove from oven and serve immediately.

Nutrition: Calories: 637, Fat: 27.7 g, Carbs: 4.5 g, Protein: 92.6 g, Sugar: 4.5 g, Sodium: 318 mg, Potassium: 1630 mg, Cholesterol: 440 mg

PORK MEATLOAF

Prep 10 minutes | **Cooking** 50 minutes | **Serving** 6

Ingredients:

- 1 cup white mushrooms, chopped
- 3 pounds lean loin pork, ground
- 2 tbsp parsley, chopped
- 2 garlic cloves, minced
- ½ cup yellow onion, chopped
- ¼ cup red bell pepper, chopped
- ½ cup almond flour
- ⅓ cup low-fat parmesan, grated
- 3 eggs

- Black pepper to the taste
- 1 tsp balsamic vinegar

Directions:

1. In a bowl, mix all the ingredients, transfer this into a loaf pan with parchment paper, and bake in the oven at 375°F for 50 minutes.
2. Leave meatloaf to cool down, slice, and serve it.

Nutrition: Calories: 2712, Fat: 144,2 g, Carbs: 17.6 g, Protein: 334.8 g, Sodium: 1519 mg, Potassium: 4079 mg, Cholesterol: 1675 mg

PORK, WATER CHESTNUTS, AND CABBAGE SALAD

Prep	Cooking	Serving
10 minutes	0 minutes	6

Ingredients:

- 1 green cabbage head, shredded
- 1 ½ cup brown rice, already cooked
- 2 cups pork roast, already cooked and shredded
- 10 ounces peas
- 8 ounces water chestnuts, drained and sliced
- 1/4 cup low-fat sour cream
- 1/4 cup avocado mayonnaise
- Black pepper pinch

Directions:

1. In a bowl, combine the cabbage with the rice, shredded meat, peas, chestnuts, sour cream, mayo, and black pepper, toss and serve cold.

Nutrition: Calories: 4833, Fat: 390.2 g, Fiber: 44.9 g, Carbs: 226.1 g, Protein: 83.8 g, Sodium: 842 mg, Potassium: 3465 mg, Cholesterol: 365 mg

RAVAGING BEEF POT ROAST

Prep	Cooking	Serving
10 minutes	75 minutes	4

Ingredients:

- 2 pounds beef roast
- 4 ounces mushrooms, sliced
- 12 ounces beef stock
- 1 ounce onion soup mix
- 1/4 cup Italian dressing, low-sodium and low-fat

Directions:

2. Add the stock, onion soup mix, and Italian dressing in a bowl. Stir.
3. Put beef roast in a pan.
4. Add mushrooms and stock mix to the pan and cover with foil.
5. Preheat your oven to 300°F.
6. Bake for 1 hour and 15 minutes.

7. Let the roast cool.

8. Slice and serve.

9. Enjoy with the gravy on top!

Nutrition:

Calories: 1531, Fat: 73.3 g, Carbs: 13.1g, Protein: 204.8 g, Sodium: 1577 mg, Potassium 3475 mg, Cholesterol: 780.2 mg

TASTY PORK PATTIES

Prep
10 minutes

Cooking
20 minutes

Serving
4

Ingredients:

- ½ cup coconut flour
- 2 tbsp olive oil
- 2 eggs, whisked
- Black pepper to the taste
- 1 ½ pounds pork, ground
- 10 ounces low Sodium: veggie stock
- ¼ cup tomato sauce, no-salt-added
- ½ tsp paprika powder

Directions:

1. Put the flour in a bowl and the egg in another one.

2. Mix the pork with black pepper and a pinch of paprika, shape medium patties out of this mix, dip them in the egg, and then dredge in flour.

3. Heat a pan with the oil over medium-high heat, add the patties, and cook them for 5 minutes on each side.

4. In a bowl, combine the stock with tomato sauce and whisk.

5. Add this over the patties, cook for 10 minutes over medium heat, divide everything between plates, and serve.

Nutrition: Calories: 2105, Fat: 156.5 g, Carbs: 9.8 g, Protein: 164.4 g, Potassium 816 mg, Cholesterol: 916.3 mg

CHAPTER 10: SEAFOOD RECIPES.

BAKED FISH SERVED WITH VEGETABLES

Prep
10 minutes

Cooking
30 minutes

Serving
4

Ingredients:

- 4 haddock or cod fillets, skinless
- 2 zucchinis, sliced into thick pieces
- 2 red onions, sliced into thick pieces
- 3 large tomatoes, cut into wedges
- ¼ cup black olives pitted
- ¼ cup flavorless oil (olive, canola, or sunflower)
- 1 tbsp lemon juice
- 1 tbsp Dijon mustard
- 2 garlic cloves, minced
- ½ cup chopped parsley

Directions:

1. Heat oven to 400°F. In a large baking dish, drizzle oil over the bottom, and place the fish in the middle. Surround the fish with zucchini, tomato, onion, and olives. Drizzle more oil over the vegetables and fish—season with salt and pepper.

2. Place the baking dish in the oven. Bake for 30 minutes until the fish is flaky and the vegetables are tender. Whisk the lemon juice, garlic, mustard, and remaining oil in another bowl. Set aside.

3. Split the cooked vegetables between plates, then top with the fish. Drizzle the dressing over the vegetables and fish. Garnish with parsley.

Nutrition: Calories: 1101 ; Fat: 71,4 g; Carbs:43,1 g; Protein: 71,7 g, Cholesterol: 133.2 mg

BAKED SALMON WITH DILL 'N GARLIC

Prep 10 minutes
Cooking 15 minutes
Serving 4

Ingredients:

- 2 (8-ounce) salmon filets, skin on
- 1 tbsp avocado oil
- A pinch black pepper
- Salt to taste
- 4 tbsp fresh dill, chopped, divided
- 1 small lemon, thinly sliced into ⅛th-inch rounds
- ¼ cup hummus
- 2 tbsp lemon juice
- 2 garlic cloves, minced

Directions:

1. Lightly grease a non-stick baking dish with cooking spray and preheat the oven to 400°F.

2. Place the fish on a baking sheet and drizzle with oil. Season with pepper and salt. Top the salmon with thinly sliced lemon.

3. Pop in the oven and roast for 15 minutes or until flaky.

4. Meanwhile, make the dill-garlic sauce by pulsing in a blender the garlic, half of the dill, and lemon juice until creamy. Stir in hummus.

5. Serve salmon topped with dill-garlic sauce and a sprinkle of chopped Dill to garnish.

Nutrition: Calories: 694 ; Protein: 47,9 g; Carbs: 15,6 g; Fat: 48,8 g; Cholesterol: 125 mg

CILANTRO LIME SALMON BOWLS

Prep 10 minutes **Cooking** 10 minutes **Serving** 4

Ingredients:

- 1 tbsp olive oil
- 1 pound salmon fillet, sliced into 4 pieces
- 3 red bell peppers, seeded and julienned
- ⅓ cup lime juice
- 2 tsp honey, organic
- Salt and pepper to taste
- 4 cups brown rice
- 1 avocado, pitted and thinly sliced

- 2 tbsp chopped cilantro

- Lime wedges

Directions:

1. Heat oil in a skillet over medium-high heat and sear the salmon on all sides for 5 minutes each. Set aside.

2. Using the same skillet, sauté the bell peppers for 3 minutes, then set aside.

3. Mix the dressing in a bowl with the lime juice, honey, salt, and pepper.

4. Assemble the salmon bowl.

5. Put a cup of rice in a bowl and add one fillet and bell peppers. Garnish with avocado slices, chopped cilantro, and lime wedges.

6. Drizzle with the dressing.

Nutrition: Calories: 4077 ; Carbs: 712,7 g; Protein: 86,9 g; Fats: 97,4 g; Cholesterol: 35 mg

EASY SHRIMP

Prep
10 minutes

Cooking
15 minutes

Serving
4

Ingredients:

- 1 pound cooked shrimp

- 1 pack mixed frozen vegetables (0,5 oz)

- 1 garlic clove, minced

- 1 tsp butter or margarine

- ♟ 1 tsp soy sauce
- ♟ ¼ cup water
- ♟ 1 pack noodles
- ♟ ½ tsp ground ginger

Directions:

1. In a large skillet, melt the butter. Add the minced garlic and sweat it for 1 minute. Add the shrimp and vegetables to the skillet—season with salt, pepper, and ginger.

2. Cover and simmer for 5 - 10 minutes, until the shrimp turns pink and the vegetables are tender.

3. Boil water in a separate pot; once it is boiling, cook the noodles accordingly to the cooking time written on the pack.

4. Transfer the noodles to the skillet, retaining the cooking water, with the shrimp and vegetables using a scoop or tongs, and add the soy sauce. Add some cooking water if the mix is too dry.

5. Mix, then serve immediately.

Nutrition: Calories: 582; Fat: 14 g; Carbs: 82.2 g; Protein: 32.1 g, Cholesterol: 800 mg

FLOUNDER WITH TOMATOES AND BASIL

Prep
10 minutes

Cooking
20 minutes

Serving
4

Ingredients:

- 1 pound cherry tomatoes
- 4 garlic cloves, sliced
- 2 tbsp extra-virgin olive oil
- 2 tbsp lemon juice
- 2 tbsp basil, cut into ribbons
- ½ tsp Kosher salt
- ¼ tsp freshly ground black pepper
- 4 (5- to 6-ounce) flounder fillets

Directions:

1. Preheat the oven to 425°F.
2. Mix the tomatoes, garlic, olive oil, lemon juice, basil, salt, and black pepper in a baking dish—Bake for 5 minutes.
3. Remove, then arrange the flounder on top of the tomato mixture. Bake until the fish is opaque and flakes, depending on thickness, for 10 to 15 minutes.
4. At halfway through, put the cherry tomato mix on top of the fish to keep it moisturized and to let the flavor penetrate the fish,

Nutrition: Calories: 882; Fat: 42,2 g; Carbs: 11,7 g; Protein: 113,7 g, Cholesterol: 328 m

GARLIC AND TOMATOES ON MUSSELS

Prep 10 minutes | **Cooking** 15 minutes | **Serving** 2

Ingredients:

- ¼ cup white wine
- ½ cup water
- 3 Roma tomatoes, chopped
- 2 garlic cloves, minced
- 1 bay leaf
- 1 pound mussels, scrubbed
- ½ cup fresh parsley, chopped
- 1 tbsp oil
- Pepper

Directions:

1. Heat a pot on medium-high heat for 3 minutes. Add oil and stir around to coat the pot with oil. Sauté the garlic, bay leaf, and tomatoes for 5 minutes.

2. Add the remaining ingredients except for parsley and mussels. Mix well.

3. Add mussels. Cover and boil for 5 minutes.

4. Serve with a sprinkle of parsley, and discard any unopened mussels.

Nutrition: Calories: 305; Fat: 18.5 g; Carbs: 11.5 g; Protein: 14.9 g, Cholesterol: 254 mg

GINGER SESAME SALMON

Prep 15-60 minutes
Cooking 5 minutes
Serving 2

Ingredients:

- 4 ounces salmon
- ⅛ cup low-sodium soy sauce
- 2 tbsp balsamic vinegar
- ½ tsp sesame oil
- 2 inch chunk ginger, peeled and grated
- 1 garlic clove, minced
- 1 tsp flavorless oil (olive, canola, or sunflower)
- 1 tsp sesame seeds
- 1 tsp spring onion, thinly sliced

Directions:

1. Combine the soy sauce, balsamic vinegar, sesame oil, garlic, and ginger in a glass dish; place the salmon in the container. Cover and marinate for 15 - 60 minutes in the fridge.

2. In a nonstick skillet, heat 1 teaspoon of oil. Sauté the fish until it becomes firm and golden on each side. Sprinkle the sesame seeds in the pan—heat for 1 minute. Serve immediately. Garnish with spring onion.

Nutrition: Calories: 452; Fat: 37.7 g; Carbs: 4.2 g; Protein: 24.1 g, Cholesterol: 63 mg

GREEN GODDESS CRAB SALAD WITH ENDIVE

Prep
10 minutes

Cooking
0 minutes

Serving
4

Ingredients:

- ½ pound lump crabmeat
- ⅔ cup plain Greek yogurt
- 3 tbsp fat-free mayonnaise
- 3 tbsp fresh chives, chopped, plus extra for garnish
- 3 tbsp fresh parsley, chopped, plus extra for garnish
- 3 tbsp fresh basil, chopped, plus extra for garnish
- 1 lemon, zest
- 1 lemon, juiced
- ¼ tsp freshly ground black pepper
- 4 endives, ends cut off, and leaves separated

Directions:

1. In a medium bowl, combine the crab, yogurt, mayonnaise, chives, parsley, basil, lemon zest, lemon juice, salt, and black pepper until well combined.

2. Place the endive leaves on 4 salad plates. Divide the crab mixture evenly on top of the endive. Garnish with additional herbs, if desired.

Nutrition: Calories: 506; Fat: 28.7 g; Carbs: 11.5 g; Protein: 50.4 g, Cholesterol: 175 mg

GRILLED HALIBUT AND FRUIT SALSA

Prep
10 minutes

Cooking
10 minutes

Serving
4

Ingredients:

For the salsa:

- 2 Jalapeños, seeded and minced
- 1 garlic clove, minced
- 1 ⅓ cup diced papaya or mango (about 1 pound, 454 g)
- 1 red bell pepper, diced
- ⅓ cup thinly sliced scallions
- ¼ cup lime juice
- 2 tbsp chopped cilantro

For the fish:

- ½ tsp paprika
- 1 garlic clove, minced
- ½ tsp freshly ground pepper
- 4 (6-ounce/170-g) skinless halibut fillets
- 1 tbsp lemon juice
- 1 tbsp olive oil
- Cooking spray

Directions:

For the salsa:

1. Put all the ingredients in a medium bowl and stir to combine.

For the fish:

1. In a large baking dish, stir the olive oil, garlic, lemon juice, paprika, and pepper. Add the fish to the mixture, turn to coat, and let stand for 10 minutes.

2. Spray a grill pan with cooking spray and heat to medium-high heat.

3. Remove the fish from the marinade, discard it, and place it on the hot grill pan. Cook for about 3 minutes per side until the desired degree of doneness is reached. Serve topped with salsa.

Nutrition: Calories: 418; Fat: 20.2 g; Carbs: 19.5 g; Protein: 39.4 g, Cholesterol: 333.2 mg

PAN-GRILLED FISH STEAKS

Prep 10 minutes | **Cooking** 10 minutes | **Serving** 4

Ingredients:

- 1 tbsp olive oil
- 1 garlic clove, minced
- 2 fillets halibut
- 1 tsp dried basil
- 1 tsp black pepper

- 1 tbsp lemon juice, freshly squeezed
- 1 tbsp fresh parsley, chopped

Directions:

1. Heat oil in a skillet over medium heat and sauté the garlic until fragrant.
2. Stir in the halibut and sear all sides for 2 minutes each.
3. Add the basil, pepper, and lemon juice.
4. Continue cooking until the liquid almost evaporates. Flip the fillet.
5. Cook for 5 more minutes.
6. Garnish with parsley before serving.

Nutrition: Calories: 791; Carbs: 2.8 g; Protein: 51.6 g; Fats: 63.7 g; Cholesterol: 240 mg

PESTO SHRIMP PASTA

Prep 10 minutes | **Cooking** 12 minutes | **Serving** 4

Servings: 4

Ingredients:

- 1 cup dried orzo
- 4 tsp packaged pesto sauce mix
- 2 tbsp olive oil, divided
- 1 pound medium shrimp, thawed

- ♟ 1 medium zucchini, halved lengthwise and sliced
- ♟ 1 lemon, halved
- ♟ ⅛ tsp coarse salt
- ♟ ⅛ tsp freshly cracked pepper
- ♟ 1 ounce shaved Parmesan cheese

Directions:

1. Mix 3 teaspoons of the pesto mix and 1 tablespoon of olive oil in a bowl, then add the shrimp. Let it marinate while you prepare the rest of the recipe.

2. Sauté zucchini in a big skillet over moderate heat for 1 to 2 minutes, stirring repeatedly. Put the pesto-marinated shrimp in the skillet and cook for 5 minutes

3. Cook the orzo pasta following package directions. Drain, reserving ¼ cup of the pasta cooking water.

4. Put the cooked pasta in the skillet with the zucchini and shrimp mix. Stir in the kept pasta water until absorbed, grating up any seasoning in the bottom of the pan. Season with pepper and salt. Squeeze the lemon over the pasta. Top with Parmesan, then serve.

Nutrition: Calories: 1253, Fat: 63.3 g, Sodium: 353 mg, Carbs: 130.8 g, Protein: 40.2 g, Potassium: 454 mg, Cholesterol: 800 mg

SALMON AVOCADO SALAD

Prep	Cooking	Serving
10 minutes	10 minutes	4

Ingredients:

- 12 ounces salmon fillet
- Salt and pepper to taste
- ½ avocado, thinly sliced
- ¼ cucumber, thinly sliced
- A dash lemon juice
- A pinch dill weed, chopped
- 2 tsp capers

Directions:

1. Preheat the grill to medium.
2. Season the salmon with salt and pepper to taste.
3. Grill the salmon for 5 minutes on each side. Set aside and allow to cool.
4. Once cooled, flake the salmon using two forks.
5. Place in a bowl and toss together with the other ingredients.
6. Season with more salt and pepper if desired.

Nutrition: Calories: 879; Carbs: 7.3 g; Protein: 68.2 g; Fats: 64.1 g; Cholesterol: 119 mg

SALMON WITH DILL AND LEMON

Prep
10 minutes

Cooking
15 minutes

Serving
2

Ingredients:

- 300g salmon fillet, cut into 2 equal portions
- Pepper to taste
- 2 lemons, juice extracted
- 2 sprigs fresh dill, chopped
- Cooking spray

Directions:

1. Preheat oven to 400°F.
2. Lightly grease an oven-safe dish with cooking spray.
3. Place salmon on the dish, skin side down.
4. Pour lemon juice, season generously with pepper, and top with dill.
5. Place in oven and bake for 12 to 15 minutes or until flaky.
6. Let salmon rest for 5 minutes.
7. Serve and enjoy.

Nutrition: Calories: 590; Carbs: 8.0 g; Protein: 56.6 g; Fats: 36.9 g; Cholesterol: 105 mg

SALMON WRAP

Prep
10 minutes

Cooking
0 minutes

Serving
1

Ingredients:

- 2 ounces low-salt Smoked Salmon
- 2 tsp low-fat cream cheese
- ½ medium-sized red onion, finely sliced
- ½ tsp fresh basil or dried basil
- A pinch pepper
- ½ cup arugula leaves
- 1 homemade wrap or any whole-meal tortilla

Directions:

1. Heat the wrap or tortilla in a heated pan or oven. Combine cream cheese, basil, and pepper, and spread on the tortilla. Top with salmon, arugula, and sliced onion. Roll up and slice. Serve and enjoy!

Nutrition: Calories: 427; Fat: 17,4 g; Carbs: 40 g; Protein: 27,9 g, Cholesterol: 15 mg

SHRIMP AND AVOCADO SALAD

Prep 10 minutes | **Cooking** 6 minutes | **Serving** 4

Ingredients:

- 1 pound shrimp, shelled and deveined
- 2 tomatoes, finely chopped
- 1 bunch cilantro, chopped
- 1 red onion, chopped finely
- 2 avocados, sliced thinly
- 2 tbsp lemon juice

Directions:

1. Steam the shrimp for 6 minutes. Set aside and allow to cool.
2. In a bowl, combine the rest of the ingredients.
3. Toss in the shrimp and gently stir.
4. Allow chilling in the fridge before serving

Nutrition: Calories: 1190; Carbs: 24.2 g; Protein: 37.3 g; Fat: 105 g; Cholesterol: 172 mg

SIMPLE TUNA AND CUCUMBER SALAD

Prep
10 minutes

Cooking
6 minutes

Serving
2

Ingredients:

- ½ pound tuna fillet
- ¼ tsp pepper
- ½ tsp salt
- 1 large cucumber, peeled and sliced
- 1 radish, peeled and sliced
- 1 medium-sized tomato, cubed
- 1 red onion, cubed
- 2 tbsp lemon juice
- 1 thumb-size ginger, grated

Directions:

1. Season the tuna with pepper.
2. Heat a skillet over medium flame and sear the tuna fillet for 3 minutes on each side. Slice the tuna into cubes and set aside.
3. In a mixing bowl, combine the rest of the ingredients and toss in the sliced tuna.
4. Season with pepper.

Nutrition: Calories: 179; Carbs: 16.7 g; Protein: 15.8 g; Fat: 5.4 g; Cholesterol: 35 mg

ROASTED VEGGIE AND LEMON PEPPER SALMON

Prep 10 minutes | **Cooking** 20 minutes | **Serving** 4

Ingredients:

- 1 carrot, peeled and julienned
- 1 red bell pepper, julienned
- 1 zucchini, julienned
- ½ lemon, sliced thinly
- 1 tsp pepper & 1 tsp salt
- ½ pound salmon filet with skin on
- A dash tarragon

Directions:

1. Preheat the oven to 400°F.
2. Place the salmon skin side down on a tray with parchment paper. Season with pepper and half of the salt, and place the slices of lemon on top
3. Add salmon skin side down in a tray and season with pepper. Add the slices of lemon on top.
4. Place the julienned vegetables on the salmon and season with tarragon and the remaining salt.
5. Bake in the oven for 20 minutes, until the vegetables and the salmon are fully cooked.
6. Let it rest for 5 minutes and serve

Nutrition: Calories: 1057; Fat: 60.9 g; Carbs: 29.7g; Protein: 97.8g, Cholesterol: 121 mg

STIR-FRIED SESAME SHRIMP

Prep
30 minutes

Cooking
15 minutes

Serving
3

Ingredients:

- ¾ cup fish broth, low sodium
- ⅛ cup cornstarch
- ½ pound sugar snap peas
- 1 tbsp teriyaki sauce
- 3 green onions, sliced
- 1 red bell pepper, sliced into thin strips
- 2 tsp sesame oil
- ¼ tsp ground black pepper
- 1 tbsp sesame seeds
- 1 garlic clove, minced
- ¼ tsp cayenne pepper
- ¼ tsp ground ginger
- 1 pound medium shrimp, peeled and deveined

Directions:

1. Mix black pepper, sesame seeds, cayenne, ginger, and shrimp in a large bowl. Mix well and let it marinate for at least 30 minutes.

2. When ready, place a nonstick saucepan on medium-high heat.

3. Add oil and heat for a minute. Swirl to coat pot.

4. Add the green onions and bell pepper. Stir fry for 4 minutes.

5. Add the shrimp, peas, and teriyaki sauce. Stir fry for 5 minutes or until shrimp is slightly opaque.

6. In a bowl, mix broth and cornstarch. Pour into pot and mix well.

7. Continue mixing and cooking until the sauce has thickened.

8. Serve and enjoy.

Nutrition: Calories: 731; Carbs: 72.8 g; Protein: 34.1 g; Fats: 33.9 g; Cholesterol: 150 mg

CHAPTER 11: VEGAN AND VEGETARIAN RECIPES.

ALMOND NOODLES WITH CAULIFLOWER

Prep 10 minutes | **Cooking** 10 minutes | **Serving** 2

Ingredients:

- 8 ounces (230 g) brown rice noodles
- 4 cups cauliflower florets (from about 2 large heads)
- ½ cup Greek yogurt
- 3 tbsp almond butter
- 2 tbsp apple cider
- 2 tbsp low-sodium soy sauce
- 1 tbsp ground fennel
- ½ tsp crushed red pepper flakes

Directions:

1. Pour 6-8 cups of water into a medium pot and boil over medium-high heat. When boiling, add the rice noodles and cook following package instructions—usually 4 to 5 minutes, or until soft.

2. Add the cauliflower florets to the cooking water and cook for a further minute. Drain the noodles and cauliflower and set aside.

3. Mix the Greek yogurt, almond butter, apple cider, soy sauce, fennel, and crushed red pepper flakes in a large pot over low heat and stir for about 2 minutes to combine the ingredients.

4. Add the noodle and cauliflower mixture to the almond sauce and combine using a tong.

5. Serve warm.

Nutrition: Calories: 1269; Fat: 41.3 g; Carbs: 181.7 g; Protein: 40.3 g, Cholesterol: 15 mg

BLACK BEANS BURGERS

Prep 10 minutes

Cooking 20 minutes

Serving 4

Ingredients:

- Nonstick cooking spray
- 2 tbsp extra-virgin olive oil, divided
- ½ large green bell pepper, coarsely chopped
- ½ small onion, coarsely chopped
- 3 garlic cloves, peeled
- 1 large egg
- 1 tbsp ground cumin
- ½ tsp garlic powder
- ¼ tsp paprika
- 1 tsp freshly ground black pepper

- ½ tsp salt
- ½ cup dried unseasoned bread crumbs
- 1 (15-ounce) can no-salt-added black beans, drained and rinsed

Directions:

1. Preheat the oven to 375°F. Coat a sheet pan with cooking spray.
2. Heat 1 tablespoon of oil in a big skillet over medium heat. Bell pepper, onion, and garlic may all be added and sautéed until tender.
3. Combine the egg, 1 tablespoon of the remaining oil, the cumin, garlic powder, paprika, black pepper, and salt in a small bowl.
4. Combine the sautéed vegetables, bread crumbs, and egg mixture in a food processor and pulse everything together. Add the black beans and pulse, leaving some bigger chunks of beans.
5. Divide the mixture into 4 portions and form into patties. Put the patties on the prepared sheet pan and bake for 10 minutes on each side.

Nutrition: Calories: 1308; Fat: 44,7 g; Carbs: 174.9 g; Protein: 52 g; Cholesterol: 223 mg

BUCKWHEAT WITH POTATOES AND KALE

Prep 10 minutes | **Cooking** 20 minutes | **Serving** 4

Ingredients:

- 1 tbsp coconut oil
- ½ cup buckwheat groats
- 2 cups cubed sweet potatoes
- 2 cups chopped kale, thoroughly washed and stemmed
- 1 yellow onion, chopped
- 2 garlic cloves, minced
- 2 tsp ground cumin
- 1 cup lentils, rinsed
- 6 cups vegetable broth
- 1 tsp salt
- ½ tsp freshly ground black pepper

Directions:

1. Add the coconut oil to a large pot, and melt over medium-high heat. Stir in the sweet potatoes, onion, garlic, and cumin. Sauté for 5 minutes.

2. Stir in the buckwheat groats, lentils, vegetable broth, salt, and pepper. Bring to a boil, simmer the heat, and cover the pot. Cook until the sweet potatoes, buckwheat, and lentils are tender, about 15 minutes.

3. Take the pot off the heat. Stir in the kale to combine. Cover the pot and let it sit for 5 minutes; serve.

Nutrition: Calories: 1749 ; Fat: 29 g; Carbs: 302,3 g; Protein: 69,6 g, Cholesterol: 0 mg

BUTTERNUT SQUASH, LENTILS, AND SPINACH GRATIN

Prep	Cooking	Serving
10 minutes	20 minutes	4

Ingredients:

- 1 tbsp coconut oil
- 2 garlic cloves, minced
- 1 onion, peeled and chopped
- 1 small butternut squash, peeled, seeded, and cut into ½-inch cubes
- 4 cups packed spinach
- 1 (15-ounce, 425 g) can lentils, drained and rinsed
- 1 tsp salt
- ½ tsp freshly ground black pepper
- 1 (13.5-ounce, 383 g) can coconut milk
- 1½ or 2 cups (360 ml to 480 ml) vegetable broth
- ¼ cup chopped fresh parsley
- ½ cup chopped toasted walnuts
- 2 tbsp chopped fresh sage

Directions:

1. Preheat the oven to 375°F (190°C).
2. Melt the coconut oil in a large ovenproof skillet over high heat. Add the garlic and onion. Sauté for 3 minutes.
3. Add the butternut squash, salt, spinach, and pepper. Sauté for another 3 minutes.
4. Stir in the coconut milk and just enough vegetable broth to cover the squash. Boil the liquid.
5. Add the parsley, lentils, and sage. Stir to combine.
6. Put the skillet in the preheated oven and bake the casserole for 15 to 20 minutes until the squash is tender.
7. Transfer the casserole to a dish and serve it garnished with walnuts.

Nutrition: Calories: 2008, Carbs: 112,5 g, Protein: 64,9 g, Fat: 144,3 g, Fiber: 39,4 g, Cholesterol: 0 mg

CAULIFLOWER MASHED "POTATOES"

Prep: 10 minutes

Cooking: 10 minutes

Serving: 4

minutes

Servings: 4

Ingredients:

- 16 cup water (enough to cover cauliflower)
- 1 head cauliflower (about 3 pounds), trimmed and cut into florets
- 4 garlic cloves
- 1 tbsp olive oil
- ¼ tsp salt
- ⅛ tsp freshly ground black pepper
- 2 tsp dried parsley

Directions:

1. Bring a pot of water to a boil. Add the garlic and cauliflower. Cook the cauliflower for 10 minutes or until it is easily pierced with a fork. Drain

2. In a pan on medium heat, cook the garlic with the olive oil for about 3 minutes. When it starts to golden, add the cooked cauliflower and sauté for another 2 minutes.

3. Place the garlic and cauliflower in a food processor or blender. Purée till smooth after adding the salt and pepper,

4. Remove and put into a serving bowl, add the parsley, and mix until combined.

5. Garnish with additional olive oil, if desired. Serve immediately.

6. If you don't have a food processor or blender, you can make this dish just as traditional mashed potatoes using a potato masher or hand blender.

Nutrition: Calories: 485; Fat: 17,8 g; Carbs: 37,7 g; Protein: 43,6 g, Cholesterol: 0 mg

CAULIFLOWER, SPINACH, AND SWEET POTATO LASAGNA

Prep 10 minutes | **Cooking** 20 minutes | **Serving** 4

Ingredients:

- 12 cups spinach (about 2 pounds, 907 g)
- 2 to 3 large sweet potatoes (about 2 pounds, 907 g), peeled and cut into ½-inch rounds
- 2 large cauliflower heads, cut into florets
- ¼ cup pine nuts, toasted
- Unsweetened plain almond milk, as needed
- 3 tbsp nutritional yeast, optional
- ½ tsp ground nutmeg
- 1 ½ tsp salt
- 1 large yellow onion, peeled and diced small
- 4 garlic cloves, peeled and minced
- 1 tbsp minced thyme
- ½ cup finely chopped basil

- 12 ounces (340 g) lasagna sheets, cooked, drained, and rinsed until cool
- Salt and freshly ground black pepper

Directions:

1. Put the sweet potatoes in a steamer basket and steam for 6 minutes until tender but not mushy. Rinse until cool, then drain them and set aside.

2. Steam the cauliflower for 6 to 8 minutes until very tender. Mix the cauliflower and pine nuts in a blender, and puree until creamy, adding almond milk if needed. Add the puree to a large bowl and stir in the nutmeg, nutritional yeast, and salt. Set aside.

3. Put the onion in a large skillet and sauté for 10 minutes over medium heat. Add the thyme, garlic, basil, and spinach, and cook for 4 to 5 minutes until the spinach wilts.

4. Combine with the cauliflower puree and mix well. Season with additional salt and pepper.

5. Preheat the oven to 350°F

6. Pour 1 cup of the cauliflower mixture into the bottom of a baking dish. Add a layer of lasagna sheet; put a layer of sweet potatoes on top of the noodles. Pour another layer of the cauliflower mixture over the sweet potatoes.

7. Top with another layer of lasagna sheet, followed by a layer of sweet potatoes. Add another layer of the cauliflower mixture. Top with a final layer of lasagna sheet and the remaining cauliflower sauce.

8. Cover with aluminum foil and bake for 30 minutes. Uncover and bake for 15 more minutes. Set aside for 15 minutes before serving.

Nutrition: Calories: 2730, Carbs: 443,7 g, Protein: 152 g, Fat: 38,7 g, Fiber: 98,9 g, Cholesterol: 0 m

CAULIFLOWER-CREAM PASTA WITH MINT

Prep 10 minutes | **Cooking** 25 minutes | **Serving** 4

Ingredients:

- 1 medium head cauliflower, cut into florets
- 2 cups (480 ml) vegetable stock or low-sodium vegetable broth
- 1 zucchini, peeled and diced
- 1 small acorn squash, peeled, halved, seeded, and cut into ½-inch cubes
- 1 pound (450 g) whole-grain penne, cooked according to package directions, drained, and kept warm
- 1 medium red bell pepper, seeded and diced
- 3 garlic cloves, smashed and skin removed
- 3 minced mint sprigs
- Salt and freshly ground black pepper to taste

Directions:

1. Mix the cauliflower and vegetable stock in a medium saucepan and bring it to a boil. Cook over medium heat for 10 minutes or until the cauliflower is very soft.

2. Turn off the heat and remove the pan, place it in a food processor, and process until smooth and creamy. Set aside.

3. Add the zucchini, squash, and red pepper, and sauté over medium heat for 7 to 8 minutes in a large saucepan. Add the garlic and the mint and cook for 5 to 6 minutes or until the squash is soft.

4. Pour in the cauliflower puree and cooked pasta, and toss until well combined. Sprinkle with salt and pepper to taste.

Nutrition: Calories: 1121, Protein: 68,6 g, Fat: 8 g, Carbs: 193,3 g, Fiber: 50,6 g, Cholesterol: 0 mg

CHICKPEA BOWLS WITH TAHINI SAUCE

Prep 10 minutes

Cooking 10 minutes

Serving 3

Ingredients:

- ⅓ cup tahini
- 2 large lemons, juiced
- 1 tsp honey
- 3 tbsp extra-virgin olive oil, divided
- 2 tbsp water, plus 1¼ cup
- 2 (15-ounce) cans no-salt-added chickpeas, drained and rinsed
- ½ tsp ground cumin
- ½ tsp freshly ground black pepper
- 1 cup whole wheat couscous
- ¼ cup finely chopped fresh parsley

- 2 small cucumbers, peeled and chopped
- 1 pint cherry tomatoes, halved
- 1 large green bell pepper, chopped
- 1 medium onion, chopped

Directions:

1. Combine the tahini, honey, lemon juice, and 1 tablespoon of oil in a small bowl. 2 tablespoons of water should be whisked in until the mixture is creamy. Place aside.

2. Combine the chickpeas, 1 tablespoon of oil, cumin, and black pepper in a medium bowl.

3. Bring the water to a boil in a medium saucepan. Once it is boiling, add the couscous, remove it from the heat, cover and give it a five-minute rest. The couscous will absorb the water and will cook. Add then the parsley and the last tablespoon of oil, and fluff.

4. Combine the cucumbers, tomatoes, bell pepper, onion, couscous, and chickpea mixture in a large bowl. Add the tahini sauce and mix well. Serve

Nutrition: Calories: 1770; Fat: 90.5 g; Carbs: 182.4 g; Protein: 56.7 g; Cholesterol: 0 mg

EASY BASIC TABLE SALAD

Prep 10 minutes | **Cooking** 0 minutes | **Serving** 2

Ingredients:

- 1 Romaine lettuce head, coarsely chopped
- ½ cup sliced yellow onion (about ½ medium onion)
- ½ –1 zucchini, cut in quarters
- 1 cup halved grape tomatoes
- 1/3 cup almond butter
- 1 lemon, juiced
- Salt to taste
- 1 cup pressed and diced extra-firm tofu added in step 1
- 1 peach, pitted and diced
- Sprinkle of nutritional yeast
- 2 tbsp toasted sesame

Directions:

1. Mix the lettuce, onion, zucchini, tofu, peach, nutritional yeast, sesame, and tomatoes in a large bowl.
2. Mix the almond butter with the lemon and a bit of water, if needed, to make a creamy dressing.

3. Add the dressing to the salad and salt, then toss to coat.

Nutrition: Calories: 911; Fat: 75.6 g; Carbs: 28.4 g; Protein: 29.1 g, Cholesterol: 0 mg

GARLIC LOVERS HUMMUS

Prep	Cooking	Serving
5 minutes	0 minutes	2

Ingredients:

- 3 tbsp freshly squeezed lemon juice
- All-purpose salt-free seasoning
- 3 tbsp sesame tahini
- 4 garlic cloves
- 15 ounces no-salt-added garbanzo beans
- 2 tbsp olive oil

Directions:

1. Drain garbanzo beans and rinse well.
2. Place all the ingredients in a food processor and pulse until smooth.
3. Serve immediately or cover and refrigerate until serving.

Nutrition: Calories: 1113, Fat: 67 g, Carbs: 88.5 g, Protein: 39 g, Cholesterol: 0 m

GRILLED CAULIFLOWER WITH SPICY LENTIL SAUCE

Prep 15 minutes

Cooking 75 minutes

Serving 4

Ingredients:

- 2 medium cauliflower heads
- 2 medium shallots, peeled and minced
- ½ cup green lentils, cooked and rinsed
- 2 cups (480 ml) low-sodium vegetable broth
- Chopped parsley
- 1 garlic clove, peeled and minced
- ½ tsp minced sage
- ½ tsp ground fennel
- ½ tsp crushed red pepper flakes
- Salt and freshly ground black pepper

Directions:

1. Cut each cauliflower head halfway through the vegetable stem, then trim each half to have a 1-inch-thick cutlet. Place each piece on a baking sheet. Save the extra cauliflower florets for other uses.

2. Put the shallots in a medium saucepan, then sauté over medium heat for 10 minutes. Add the garlic, fennel, sage, crushed red pepper flakes, and lentils, and cook for 3 minutes.

3. Add the vegetable stock and boil the mixture over high heat. Low the heat to medium and cook, covered, for 45 to 50 minutes. Add water as needed to keep the mix from drying out.

4. Puree the lentil mixture using an immersion blender. Return the puree to the pan if necessary and season with salt and pepper. Keep warm.

5. Prepare the grill.

6. Place the cauliflower on the grill, then cook each side for about 7 minutes.

7. Place the grilled cauliflower on a plate and spoon the sauce over them. Garnish with chopped parsley and serve.

Nutrition: Calories: 709; Fat: 7.9 g; Carbs: 81.3 g; Protein: 77.7 g, Cholesterol: 0 mg

HEALTHY CAULIFLOWER PURÉE

Prep 10 minutes | **Cooking** 10 minutes | **Serving** 4

Ingredients:

- 1 garlic clove
- 1 cauliflower head, broken into florets
- ½ cup coconut milk
- 2 tsp salt, divided
- ¼ tsp freshly ground black pepper
- 1 tbsp extra-virgin olive oil

Directions:

1. Boil a huge pot of water over high heat. After boiling, add cauliflower, garlic cloves, and 1 tsp of salt. Cook for about 5 minutes, until the cauliflower is soft.

2. Remove the cauliflower from the pot, drain it, and put it in a large bowl. Mash with a potato masher.

3. Sprinkle the remaining 1 teaspoon of salt, pepper, and coconut milk on the mashed cauliflower. Stir well.

4. Transfer the puree to a bowl and drizzle with olive oil.

Nutrition: Calories: 603; Fat: 38.3 g; Carbs: 30.2 g; Protein: 34.2 g, Cholesterol: 0 mg

BASIL PESTO

Prep	Cooking	Serving
10 minutes	0 minutes	4

Ingredients:

- ½ cup fresh basil leaves
- ½ cup freshly grated Parmesan cheese
- ¼ cup extra-virgin olive oil
- ⅓ cup pine nuts or walnuts
- 3 garlic cloves, minced
- ¼ tsp salt, or more to taste
- ⅛ tsp freshly ground black pepper or more to taste

Directions:

1. Put all the ingredients, except the oil, into a food processor.

2. Start pulsing the food processor several times to start blitzing the ingredients.

3. Then keep the food processor running and slowly pour the olive oil in until the pesto is blitzed and the oil is incorporated.

4. Don't blitz too much to keep the pesto of bright green.

Nutrition: Calories: 894; Fat: 84.4 g; Carbs: 4.6 g; Protein: 29.1 g, Cholesterol: 44 mg

PAN FRIED GREEN BEANS

Prep 10 minutes | **Cooking** 15 minutes | **Serving** 4

Ingredients:

- 2 tbsp olive oil
- 2 tsp sweet paprika
- 1 lemon, juiced
- 2 tbsp basil pesto
- 1 pound trimmed and halved green beans
- ¼ tsp black pepper
- 1 sliced red onion

Directions:

1. Heat the oil to the pan over medium heat, add the onions, stir, and fry for 5 minutes.

2. Add the beans and the remaining ingredients, toss, cook over medium heat for 10 minutes, divide between plates, and serve.

Nutrition: Calories: 447, Fat: 35.4 g, Carbs: 22.8 g, Protein: 9.1 g, Sugars: 22.8 g, Cholesterol: 0 mg

ROASTED CHICKPEAS

Prep	Cooking	Serving
5 minutes	30-40 minutes	4

Ingredients:

- 1 (15-ounce can) chickpeas, drained and rinsed
- ½ tsp olive oil
- 2 tsp favorite herbs or spice blend
- ¼ tsp salt

Directions:

1. Preheat the oven to 400°F.

2. Wrap a rimmed baking sheet with paper towels, place the chickpeas in an even layer, and blot with more paper towels until most of the liquid is absorbed.

3. In a medium bowl, gently toss the chickpeas and olive oil until combined. Sprinkle the mixture with the herbs and salt and toss again.

4. Place the chickpeas on the baking sheet and spread in an even layer. Bake for 30 to 40 minutes, until crunchy and golden brown. Stir halfway through. Serve.

Nutrition: Calories: 604 g, Fat: 17.8 g, Sodium: 5 mg, Carbs: 79.6 g, Protein: 31.5 g, Cholesterol: 0 mg

ROASTED EGGPLANT SANDWICHES

Prep
10 minutes

Cooking
30 minutes

Serving
2

Ingredients:

- Nonstick cooking spray (optional)
- 1 small eggplant, cut crosswise into ⅓-inch-thick slices
- 1 tbsp extra-virgin olive oil
- ¼ tsp freshly ground black pepper
- 1 tomato, sliced
- 1 small red onion, sliced
- ½ cup chopped fresh basil
- 2 ounces fresh burrata cheese
- 4 whole wheat bread slices

Directions:

1. Preheat the oven to 375°F. Line a sheet pan with aluminum foil or coat it with nonstick cooking spray.

2. Brush both sides of the eggplant with the oil, put on the prepared sheet pan, and season with the pepper. Roast for about 25 minutes until the skin is wrinkly and the eggplant is soft, and let cool.

3. Divide the roasted eggplant into 2 portions and place it in one partition of 2 divided storage containers. Divide the tomato, onion, and basil into the second partition. Store the burrata cheese and bread in separate containers.

4. To serve, reheat the eggplant in the microwave for 30 seconds to 1 minute. For each sandwich, toast 2 bread slices. Layer one-quarter of the cheese on a slice of toast and top with the eggplant, tomato, and onion. Add the basil and close the sandwich.

Nutrition: Calories: 1363; Fat: 70.1 g; Carbs: 35.4 g; Protein: 48.7 g; Cholesterol: 140 mg

SLOW COOKED QUINOA AND LENTILS TACOS

Prep
10 minutes

Cooking
30 minutes

Serving
6

Ingredients:

- 1 tsp smoked paprika
- 1 tsp salt
- 1 tsp onion powder
- 1 tsp garlic powder
- 1 ½ cup quinoa
- 1 ½ cup red lentils
- 6 cups vegetable stock
- 2 tbsp chopped chipotles in adobo, or more as desired
- 420g Whole-wheat tortillas
- Chopped tomatoes

Directions:

1. Add all the rinsed quinoa, the rinsed lentils, the seasonings, the stock, and the chipotle in a pot. Bring to a boil and then simmer for 30 minutes until the lentils and the quinoa are cooked. Once cooked, remove them from the heat and let them rest for 10 minutes.

2. Place the tortillas in a dry skillet and warm over medium heat. Mix the warm tortillas with the quinoa and lentils and top with the cherry tomatoes.

Nutrition: Calories: 1980; Fat: 69.4 g; Carbs: 268.2 g; Protein: 69.4 g, Cholesterol: 0 mg

STUFFED TEX-MEX BAKED POTATOES

Prep 10 minutes **Cooking** 45 minutes **Serving** 4

Ingredients:

- 2 large Idaho potatoes
- ½ cup black beans, rinsed and drained
- ¼ cup store-bought salsa
- 1 avocado, diced
- 1 tsp freshly squeezed lime juice
- ½ cup nonfat plain Greek yogurt
- ½ tsp onion powder
- ½ tsp garlic powder
- ½ tsp paprika

- ½ tsp chili powder
- ¼ cup shredded sharp Cheddar cheese

Directions:

1. Preheat the oven to 400°F. Scrub the potatoes, then slice an "X" into each top using a paring knife. Put the potatoes on the oven rack, then bake for 45 minutes until tender.

2. In a small bowl, stir the beans and salsa and set aside. Mix the avocado and lime juice in another small bowl and set aside. In a third small bowl, stir the yogurt and the spices until well blended.

3. When the potatoes are baked, carefully open them up. Top each potato with the bean and salsa mixture, avocado, seasoned yogurt, and cheddar cheese, evenly divide each component, and serve.

Nutrition: Calories: 1278, Fat: 72.7 g, Carbs: 99.1 g, Fiber: 28.8 g, Protein: 56.9 g, Sodium: 340 mg, Potassium: 3745 mg, Cholesterol: 24.2 mg

WHITE BEANS WITH SPINACH AND PAN-ROASTED TOMATOES

Prep	Cooking	Serving
10 minutes	10 minutes	4

Ingredients:

- 1 tbsp olive oil
- 4 small plum tomatoes, halved lengthwise
- 10 ounces spinach
- 2 garlic cloves, thinly sliced

- ¼ tsp freshly ground black pepper
- 1 can white beans, drained
- 1 lemon, juiced

Directions:

1. Heat the oil in a large skillet over medium-high heat. Put the tomatoes cut-side down, and cook within 3 to 5 minutes; turn and cook within 1 minute more. Transfer to a plate.

2. Reduce heat to medium and cook the garlic with the oil for about 3 minutes; add the spinach with the seasoning and cook for a few minutes, until the spinach is cooked and the water evaporates.

3. Return the tomatoes to the skillet, put the white beans and lemon juice, and toss until heated through 1 to 2 minutes.

Nutrition: Calories: 494, Fat: 19,8 g, Sodium: 1528 mg, Carbs: 48,9 g, Protein: 30,2 g, Potassium: 3707 mg, Cholesterol: 0 mg

CORIANDER FALAFEL

Prep 10 minutes | **Cooking** 10 minutes | **Serving** 4

Ingredients:

- 1 cup canned garbanzo beans
- 1 bunch parsley leaves
- 1 yellow onion, chopped
- 5 garlic cloves, minced

- 1 tsp coriander, ground
- A pinch salt and black pepper
- ¼ tsp cayenne pepper
- ¼ tsp baking soda
- ¼ tsp cumin powder
- 1 tsp lemon juice
- 3 tbsp tapioca flour
- Olive oil for frying

Directions:

1. Combine the beans with the parsley, onion, and other ingredients except for oil and flour, and pulse well in your food processor.

2. Transfer the mix to a bowl, add the flour, stir well, shape 16 balls out of this mix, and flatten them.

3. Preheat pan over medium-high heat; add the falafels, cook them for 5 minutes on both sides, put in paper towels, drain excess grease, arrange them on a platter, and serve as an appetizer.

Nutrition: Calories: 643, Carbs: 72,4 g, Fat: 34 g, Protein: 11,9 g, Sodium: 15 mg, Potassium 229 mg, Cholesterol: 0 mg

CHEESY ZUCCHINI PANCAKE

Prep
10 minutes

Cooking
5 minutes

Serving
4

Ingredients:

- 1 cup whole wheat or all-purpose flour
- 2 tsp baking powder
- ½ tsp salt
- 2 tbsp canola or vegetable oil, plus more for greasing
- 1 cup cheese
- ½ cup grated zucchini (about 1 small zucchini)
- 1 cup plant-based milk
- 1 ½ tsp vanilla extract
- 1 tbsp agave, brown sugar, or maple syrup
- ¼ tsp lemon zest
- ½ tbsp flaxseed meal
- Vegan butter

Directions:

1. Preheat a nonstick pan over medium-high heat. You can lightly grease the pan if you don't have a nonstick pan (or your nonstick pan needs more slip).

2. Combine all the ingredients in a medium bowl. Gently toss until the batter is smooth, but removing all the lumps is unnecessary.

3. Scoop out the batter using a ¼-cup measuring cup and pour it onto the preheated pan. Once bubbles begin forming in the pancake's center, turn the pancake over to cook the other side until light brown. Remove from the heat and repeat with the rest of the batter.

Nutrition: Calories: 1925, Carbs: 138,1 g, Protein: 67,8 g, Fat: 122,4 g, Fiber: 27,4 g, Cholesterol: 100 mg

HEARTY BRUSSELS AND PISTACHIO

Prep 10 minutes **Cooking** 15 minutes **Serving** 4

Ingredients:

- 1 pound brussels sprouts, tough bottom trimmed and halved lengthwise
- 4 shallots, peeled and quartered
- 1 tbsp extra-virgin olive oil
- Sea salt
- Freshly ground black pepper
- ½ cup roasted pistachios, chopped
- ½ lemon, zest
- ½ lemon, juiced

Directions:

1. Preheat your oven to 400°F

2. Take a baking sheet and line it with aluminum foil

3. Keep it on the side

4. Take a large bowl and add Brussels and shallots, and dress them with olive oil

5. Season with salt and pepper and spread veggies onto a sheet.

6. Bake for 15 minutes until slightly caramelized

7. Remove the oven and transfer to a serving bowl

8. Toss with lemon zest, lemon juice, and pistachios.

Nutrition: Calories: 941 Fat: 54,1 g Carbs: 56 g Protein: 57,4 g, Cholesterol: 0 mg

CHAPTER 12: DESSERTS

ALMOND RICE PUDDING WITH RASPBERRY SAUCE

Prep
10 minutes

Cooking
20 minutes

Serving
4

Ingredients:

- 1 (10-ounce, 283 g) bag frozen raspberries, thawed
- 2 ounces (57 g) cream cheese at room temperature
- 2 cups unsweetened vanilla almond milk
- ½ cup white rice
- ⅓ cup sugar
- ⅛ tsp salt

Directions:

1. Combine the almond milk, rice, sugar, and salt in a 3-quart slow cooker. Cover and cook on low for 20 minutes. Cooking on high will make the rice cook unevenly.
2. Add the cream cheese and stir until melted.
3. Transfer to a bowl and refrigerate until the rice pudding is chilled.
4. Place the raspberries in a blender or food processor, and blend until smooth. Pour into a bowl.
5. Stir the pudding before serving it with the raspberry sauce on top.

Nutrition: Calories: 181, Fat: 27,4 g, Sodium: 203 mg, Potassium: 943 mg, Carbs: 191 g, Cholesterol: 55 mg

BANANA CREAM AND LOW-FAT YOGURT

Prep	Cooking	Serving
10 minutes	0 minutes	4

Ingredients:

- 1 medium banana
- 1 Graham cracker
- 1 tsp fresh lemon juice
- 1 cup low-fat vanilla yogurt

Directions:

1. Slice the banana into a bowl.
2. Break the graham cracker into small pieces and add to the banana.
3. Sprinkle with lemon juice and top with yogurt.

Nutrition: Calories: 205, Protein: 9,7 g, Fat: 4,4 g, Carbs: 31,7 g, Fiber: 2,3 g, Cholesterol: 12 mg

BERRIES COBBLER

Prep 10 minutes **Cooking** 45 minutes **Serving** 4

Ingredients:

For the filling:

- 5 cups mixed berries (such as blueberries, raspberries, and strawberries)
- 2 tbsp fresh lemon juice
- ⅓ cup agave
- 3 tbsp cornstarch
- A pinch salt

For the biscuit topping:

- ½ cup (120 ml) unsweetened plant-based milk
- 1 tsp apple cider vinegar
- 1 tsp pure vanilla extract
- 1 ½ cups oat flour
- 1 tbsp baking powder
- ¼ cup agave
- ¼ tsp salt
- 3 tbsp unsweetened applesauce
- 2 tbsp almond butter

For sprinkling:

- 🎩 1 tbsp dry sweetener
- 🎩 ¼ tsp ground cinnamon

Directions:

1. Preheat the oven to 425°F (220°C). Line an 8 × 8-inch pan with parchment paper, making sure that the parchment goes up the sides of the pan, or prepare an 8 × 8-inch nonstick or silicone baking pan.

To make the filling:

1. Mix the berries, agave, cornstarch, lemon juice, and salt in a large bowl until well combined. Put the mixture in the prepared pan. Bake for 25 minutes, covered with aluminum foil.

To make the biscuit topping:

1. Whisk the apple cider vinegar and plant-based milk in a large measuring cup. Set aside to let curdle for a few minutes, then add the vanilla.
2. Sift the baking powder, oat flour, and salt in a large bowl.
3. Mix the applesauce, the agave, and the almond butter in a small bowl.
4. Combine the applesauce and flour mixture with a fork until crumbly. Add the milk mixture and stir until just moistened.

To assemble the cobbler:

1. Reduce the oven temperature to 350°F (180°C). Remove the foil from the pan and drop a spoonful of the batter over the berry filling, mix the cinnamon and dry sweetener, and sprinkle evenly over the top of the biscuit dough. Put the pan back into the oven, uncovered, and bake for another 20 minutes.
2. Take out the pan from the oven and transfer it to a cooling rack. Serve warm.

Nutrition: Calories: 638, Carbs: 152,2 g, Protein: 4,2 g, Fat: 1,7 g, Fiber: 9,7 g, Cholesterol: 0 mg

CHOCOLATE CHIP COOKIES

Prep
10 minutes

Cooking
10 minutes

Serving
4

Ingredients:

- ⅓ cup (80 ml) unsweetened applesauce
- ⅓ cup (80 ml) almond butter
- ½ cup dry sweetener
- 1 tbsp ground flaxseeds
- 2 tsp pure vanilla extract
- ¼ cup sorghum flour or whole wheat pastry flour
- ½ cup grain-sweetened chocolate chips
- 1⅓ cup oat flour
- ½ tsp baking soda
- ½ tsp salt

Directions:

1. Preheat the oven to 350°F (180°C). Line two large baking sheets with parchment paper.

2. Use a fork to beat the almond butter, dry sweetener, applesauce, and flaxseeds in a large mixing bowl. Once relatively smooth, add the vanilla.

3. Mix in the baking soda, oat flour, and salt. Add the sorghum flour and chocolate chips and combine well.

4. Drop batter onto the prepared baking sheets in about 1½-tablespoon scoops, about 2 inches apart. Flatten the cookies a bit so that they resemble thick discs. Bake for 8 to 10 minutes.

5. Remove the cookies from the oven and cool them down on the sheets for 5 minutes, then transfer them to a cooling rack to cool completely.

Nutrition: Calories: 1679, Carbs: 180 g, Protein: 42.6 g, Fat: 79.7 g, Fiber: 17.8 g, Cholesterol: 0 mg

CHOCOLATE CUPCAKES

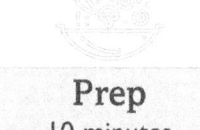

Prep 10 minutes | **Cooking** 20 minutes | **Serving** 4

Ingredients:

- 1 cup whole wheat pastry flour or spelt flour
- ⅓ cup cocoa powder, either regular unsweetened or Dutch-processed
- 2 ounces unsweetened chocolate
- 1 cup unsweetened plant-based milk
- 1 tsp apple cider vinegar
- ⅔ cup dry sweetener
- ¼ cup unsweetened applesauce
- 1 tsp pure vanilla extract
- ¾ tsp baking soda

- ½ tsp baking powder
- ¼ tsp salt

Directions:

1. Preheat the oven to 350°F (180°C). Line a 12-cup muffin pan with silicone liners or prepare a nonstick or silicone muffin pan.

2. In the microwave, melt the chocolate in a small bowl. Set aside.

3. Whisk together the vinegar and plant-based milk in a large bowl. Set aside for a few minutes until curdled. Stir in the dry sweetener, vanilla, applesauce, and melted chocolate.

4. Sift the flour, baking soda, cocoa powder, baking powder, and salt in a separate bowl. Add the mixture to the wet ingredients, half time, and whisk until no large lumps remain.

5. Scoop the batter on the prepared pan, with each cup three-quarters full. Bake for 18 to 20 minutes until a toothpick inserted into the center comes clean.

6. Remove the pan from the oven and cool down the cupcakes for at least 20 minutes, then run a knife around the edges of each cupcake carefully to remove it. The cupcakes should be completely cool before eating

Nutrition: Calories: 1491, Carbs: 207.4 g, Protein: 53.6 g, Fat: 48.4 g, Fiber: 44.6 g, Cholesterol: 0 mg

CINNAMON BAKED APPLE CHIPS

Prep	Cooking	Serving
5 minutes	120 minutes	2

Ingredients:

- 1 tsp cinnamon
- 1-2 apples

Directions:

1. Set your oven to 200°F for best results.
2. Slice the apples into thin slices using a sharp knife.
3. Throw away seeds.
4. Place apples on a baking sheet that has been lined with parchment paper.
5. Ensure that they don't overlap.
6. When finished, sprinkle apples with cinnamon.
7. Bake for one hour in the oven.
8. Until no longer moist, flip, and bake for another hour.

Nutrition: Calories: 203 Fat: 1,4 g Carbs: 46,8 g Protein: 1 g, Cholesterol: 0 mg

DATES CREAM

Prep
5 minutes

Cooking
0 minutes

Serving
4

Ingredients:

- 1 cup almond milk
- 1 banana, peeled and sliced
- 1 tsp vanilla extract
- ½ cup coconut cream
- 1 cup dates, chopped

Directions:

1. In a blender, blitz all the ingredients together until smooth. Pour into small cups and serve cold.

Nutrition: Calories: 1752 Protein: 9 g, Carbs: 82,6 g, Fat: 43,8 g, Sodium: 5 mg, Potassium: 1080 mg, Cholesterol: 0 mg

HOMEMADE PROTEIN BAR

Prep Overnight | **Cooking** 0 minutes | **Serving** 4

Ingredients:

- 1 cup peanut butter
- 4 tbsp coconut oil
- 2 scoops vanilla protein
- 1 tbsp of chocolate chips
- Stevia, to taste
- ½ tsp sea salt
- 1 tsp cinnamon

Directions:

1. Mix coconut oil with butter, protein, stevia, and salt in a dish.
2. Stir in cinnamon and chocolate chip.
3. Press the mixture firmly and refrigerate overnight until firm.
4. Cut the crust into small bars.
5. Serve and enjoy.

Nutrition: Calories: 2070, Fat: 188,6 g, Carbs: 40,3 g, Protein: 53,8 g, Fiber: 16,5 g, Cholesterol: 0 mg

SHORTBREAD COOKIES

Prep
10 minutes

Cooking
10 minutes

Serving
4

Ingredients:

- 2 ½ cups coconut flour
- 6 tbsp walnut butter
- ½ cup erythritol
- 1 tsp vanilla essence

Directions:

1. Preheat your oven to 350°F.
2. Layer a cookie sheet with parchment paper.
3. Beat butter with erythritol until fluffy.
4. Stir in vanilla essence and coconut flour. Mix well until crumbly.
5. Spoon out a tablespoon of cookie dough onto the cookie sheet.
6. Add more dough to make as many cookies as possible.
7. Bake for 15 minutes until brown.
8. Serve.

Nutrition: Calories: 2095, Fat: 162,8 g, Carbs: 127,8 g, Protein: 29,9 g, Fiber: 45,5g, Cholesterol: 0 mg

WALNUT BUTTER BARS

Prep: Overnight
Cooking: 0 minutes
Serving: 4

Ingredients:

- ¾ cup coconut flour
- 2 ounces walnut butter
- ¼ cup swerve
- ½ cup walnut butter
- ½ tsp vanilla

Directions:

1. Combine all the ingredients in a bowl.
2. Transfer this mixture into a tray, making a 1-inch layer, press firmly, and refrigerate overnight.
3. Once the mix is set, slice and serve.

Nutrition: Calories: 1612, Fat: 126 g, Carbs: 78,2 g, Protein: 41,5 g, Fiber: 23,4 g, Cholesterol: 0 mg

CARROT CAKE

Prep 15 minutes | **Cooking** 45 minutes | **Serving** 4

Ingredients:

- 1 cup whole-wheat flour
- ½ cup all-purpose flour; sifted
- ¼ cup and 2 tbsp brown sugar
- ½ tsp baking soda
- ½ tsp baking powder
- ¼ tsp ground ginger
- ½ tsp ground cinnamon
- 1 tsp grated orange zest
- 1 tbsp walnuts, finely chopped
- 1 ½ cup grated carrots
- ½ tbsp raisins
- ⅓ cup margarine; trans-fat-free, softened
- ⅓ cup low-fat milk
- 1 beaten egg whites/egg substitute equal to 1 egg
- 1 tsp vanilla extract
- ¾ tbsp orange juice

Directions:

1. Preheat the oven to 350°F.

2. Coat a 2 ½, 4 ½, 8 ½ inch loaf pan with cooking spray.

3. Combine the dry ingredients in a bowl and set aside.

4. Mix margarine and sugar in a large bowl using an electric or whisk mixer.

5. Add the milk, vanilla, egg, orange juice, raisins, carrots, and walnuts.

6. Add the dry ingredients that have been set aside. Mix thoroughly.

7. Pour the mix into the loaf pan and bake for about 45 minutes, or until a wooden pick inserted in the middle comes out clean.

8. Allow 10 minutes to cool in the pan. Remove the pan from the oven, then cool fully on a wire rack.

Nutrition: Calories: 1648, Fat: 62.3 g, Carbs: 236.2 g, Protein: 32.6 g, Saturated Fat: 13.7 g, Cholesterol: 0 mg, Sugar: 116.7 g

MANGO PANNA COTTA

Prep 10 minutes | **Cooking** 0 minutes | **Serving** 4

Ingredients:

- 2 mangoes, peeled and diced
- 1 can low-fat coconut milk (14oz)
- 2 tbsp maple syrup
- 1 lime juice

Directions:

1. Blend all the ingredients into a blender until smooth.
2. Pour mango mixture into panna cotta molds or small glasses and place in the refrigerator until set.
3. Serve chilled and enjoy.

Nutrition: Calories: 1358, Fat: 86,1 g, Carbs: 131,8 g, Protein: 13,7 g, Saturated Fat: 75,39 g, Cholesterol: 0 mg

STRAWBERRIES AND AMARETTO CREAM

Prep 60 minutes | **Cooking** 0 minutes | **Serving** 4

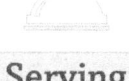

Ingredients:

- 2 cups fat-free sour cream;
- ½ cup brown sugar
- 4 cups fresh strawberries; halved
- whole strawberries for garnish
- 2 tbsp Amaretto liqueur

Directions:

1. Combine the sour cream, the liqueur, and the sugar in a small bowl.
2. Combine the sour cream mixture and halved strawberries in a large mixing bowl. Cover, then chill for 1 hour or until well cooked.
3. Fill four chilled glasses with cream and strawberries and garnish with a few whole strawberries.

Nutrition: Calories: 1579, Fat:98,4 g, Carbs: 152,7 g, Protein: 13,4 g, Saturated Fat: 58,25 g, Cholesterol: 5 mg, Sugar: 152,7 g

CHAPTER 13: A 28-DAY MEAL PLAN

	Breakfast	**Lunch**	**Dinner**	**Desserts**
DAY 1	Creamy oats banana porridge	Almond noodles with cauliflower	Buckwheat with potatoes and kale	Almond rice pudding with raspberry sauce
DAY 2	Green smoothie with berries and banana	Black bean burgers	Butternut squash, lentils, and spinach gratin	Banana cream and low-fat yogurt
DAY 3	Muesli with berries, seeds, and nuts	Shrimp and avocado salad	Lamb chops with rosemary	Chocolate chip cookies
DAY 4	Berry, walnut, and cinnamon quinoa bowl	Roasted veggie and lemon pepper salmon	Garlic lime marinated pork chops	Chocolate cupcakes
DAY 5	Berry, walnut, and cinnamon quinoa bowl	Stir-fried sesame shrimp	Grilled fennel-cumin lamb chops	Cinnamon-baked apple chips
DAY 6	Peach-cranberry sunrise muesli	Simple tuna and cucumber salad	Healthy beef cabbage	Homemade protein bar

DAY 7	Creamy chocolate-cherry smoothie	Cilantro lime salmon bowls	Citrus pork	Shortbread cookies
DAY 8	Easy strawberry kiwi smoothie	Easy shrimp	Garlic and tomatoes on mussels	Walnut butter bars
DAY 9	Fruit smoothie with Greek yogurt	Flounder with tomatoes and basil	Easy veal chops	Carrot cake
DAY 10	Ginger and carrot pear smoothie	Chickpea garlic noodle soup	Healthy meatballs	Mango panna cotta
DAY 12	Green apple and oat bran smoothie	Cream of mushroom soup	Hearty pork belly casserole	Strawberries and amaretto cream
DAY 13	Eggplant fries	Curry lentil soup	Jerk beef and plantain kabobs	Berries cobbler
DAY 14	Lemon broccoli	Flavors vegetable stew	Beef veggie pot meal	Chocolate cupcakes

DAY 15	Millet porridge	Greek lentil soup	Beef with mushrooms	Cinnamon-baked apple chips
DAY 16	Quinoa almond porridge	Garlic mushroom chicken	Healthy chicken orzo	Dates cream
DAY 17	Bell pepper pancakes	Delicious chicken tenders	Healthy cauliflower purée	Homemade protein bar
DAY 18	Coconut-berry sunrise smoothie	Asian chicken breasts	Grilled cauliflower with spicy lentil sauce	Berries cobbler
DAY 19	Bell pepper pancakes	Pesto shrimp pasta	Salmon avocado salad	Banana cream and low-fat yogurt
DAY 20	Coconut-berry sunrise smoothie	Tuscan fish stew	Thick & creamy potato soup	Chocolate chip cookies
DAY 21	Creamy chocolate-cherry smoothie	Spicy lentil chili	Garlic lover's hummus	Almond rice pudding with raspberry sauce

DAY 22	Easy strawberry kiwi smoothie	Hearty vegetable stew	Indian vegetable stew	Strawberries and amaretto cream
DAY 23	Fruit smoothie with Greek yogurt	Roasted chickpeas	Juicy chicken patties	Shortbread cookies
DAY 24	Ginger and carrot pear smoothie	Lentil veggie stew	Slow-cooked quinoa and lentils tacos	Walnut butter bars
DAY 25	Green apple and oat bran smoothie	Classic chicken	Cheesy zucchini pancake	Carrot cake
DAY 26	Quinoa almond porridge	Chicken thighs and apple mix	Chicken tortillas	Mango panna cotta
DAY 27	Green smoothie with berries and banana	White beans with spinach and pan-roasted tomatoes	Cheesy zucchini pancake	Strawberries and amaretto cream
DAY 28	Muesli with berries, seeds, and nuts	White beans with spinach and pan-roasted tomatoes	Hot chicken wings	Dates cream

CHAPTER 14: WEEKLY PLANS OF SIMPLE EXERCISES

EXERCISES EXPLAINATION

LUNGES

Maintaining a straight upper body is crucial when lunging. Maintain a comfortable posture with your face forward and shoulders back. Keep your head up.

After your posture is in order, step forward with one leg and bring your hips down. To receive the maximum benefits of the lunge, both knees must be bent at a 90-degree angle. The goal is to have both the thigh of the leg you used to move forward and the shin of the leg you maintained in place parallel to the floor. Ensure your knee does not contact the floor and maintain your weight on your heels.

It's time for you now.

The lunge comes in various forms, but mastering the basic lunge is necessary before attempting more intricate ones. You won't be able to perform any of the other lunges if you can't execute a basic lunge correctly. Start by improving your posture.

- Pro advice Take a smaller stride if your knees are being overexerted.

JUMPING JACKS

Bend your knees just a little while standing up straight, with your legs and hands at your sides. Now widen your legs and raise your arms; it should be seamless. Your feet shouldn't trail your arms in movement, and you can now restart from your starting position.

- Pro advice: To get the most out of the workout, stretch your legs wider than your shoulders.

SQUATS

Take a comfortable stance with your feet slightly apart and your back straight. The ideal position is to stand with your feet slightly outward and shoulder-width apart. You want to stare straight forward, just as with lunges. Imagine that you are going to get a punch. Feel your abdominal muscles tensing up. Keep them stiff like that.

Let's get to the fun stuff now that we've got your posture under control.

Imagine yourself sitting on a chair without arching your back. Lower, a chair. You want to squat as low as you can while maintaining parallel thighs. Keep your knees from giving way. Firm up your legs.

- Pro advice: Squats should be considered sitting backward, not merely knee bending. Instead of merely keeping it in place, you must push your butt backward.

BURPEES

As I've shown you, stoop down to the ground. Put your hands on the ground in front of you right now. Make sure that your hands and feet are at the same distance from one another. Jump back with your feet while shifting weight from your feet to your hands. Get into the plank posture. It implies that your body should be straight from your head to your ankles. Keep your back straight, and avoid lifting your hips high.

The next step is to jump into your starting position again, leap high into the air (similar to a jump squat), and then land back on your feet. You should instantly drop back as soon as you land.

- Pro advice: If you feel overwhelmed, divide things into smaller stages. Everyone, especially novices, will find this to be a challenging workout. Before combining everything into one large task, try doing smaller portions independently.

PLANKS

The simplest method to accomplish this is first to assume a pushup stance. It implies that you should keep your body upright and support yourself with your arms and toes. Go down to your elbows at this point. Your forearms will now support your weight as you continue. Maintain your neck straight so you are gazing down at the ground rather than forward. Now you are performing a plank!

Be sure to breathe consistently and evenly. You'll know you've done it long enough when your arms hang and your back slumps.

- Pro advice: This workout focuses on maintaining a straight body while breathing. If you execute things correctly, you will only gain from it. Always maintain a straight posture.

PUSHUPS

Lay down and place your hands flat on the ground. Your shoulders and hands should be slightly apart. Your hands may be used in various ways, from knuckles to gripping bars. Find out what suits you the most. I've discovered that the greatest technique to push myself up is with my knuckles.

Remember when situating your feet that the further apart they are, the more stable you will be when performing the pushup. As long as you can support yourself on your toes, it doesn't matter.

Your body should remain straight. Keep your back straight, and avoid lifting your glutes. Always maintain as much uprightness as you can.

Never let your hands extend too far from your body. It shouldn't be much wider than your shoulders—just an inch or two.

So that your arms are straight, lift yourself. Now that you're prepared start your pushups.

Push yourself back up after lowering yourself until your elbows parallel your shoulders.

- Pro advice: This advice may be helpful if you struggle to maintain a straight line. Flex your abs while clenching your glutes.

Why not attempt a bent knee pushup if you're not confident performing a regular pushup? Use your knees in place of your toes, that's all. It implies that, unlike a typical pushup, you are not engaging your lower legs.

CRUNCHES

On the floor, start by lying on your back. Now imagine yourself lying on the sand with your hands supporting your head. Your arms should form the shape of a diamond.

Things start to become intriguing at this point.

Start selling now! Imagine that you are competing in a race while riding a bicycle. Stretch your other leg straight while bringing one knee to your chest. Keep the straight leg off the floor. Touch your left knee with your right elbow while raising your left leg, and vice versa. Twist as far as necessary to touch those elbows and knees.

- Pro advice: Start slowly and firmly plant your arms and back on the floor. Just pedal for a bit to get used to it and to discover the appropriate pace for you to go at. You may add the elbows to the knees after you're at a comfortable enough level. To achieve the best benefit, keep your abdominal muscles tight.

TWISTING MOUNTAIN CLIMBERS

Start in a plank posture, like with many other excellent exercises. Put your arms in the same position as though you were performing pushups. Now alternate bringing your right knee to your left elbow. Left knee, right knee, left elbow, right elbow, right elbow, right knee, left knee, left elbow, left knee. That's all, then! You are ascending a mountain.

- Pro advice: Maintain your alignment throughout. Avoid hunching your neck or slouching your back. Your legs and feet should be the only things moving.

SIDE PLANKS

There are a lot of nice, straightforward things in life. Black coffee, chocolate, vanilla ice cream, even the side plank.

Stretch your legs out straight while lying on your side. Push your upper body up while keeping your forearm flat on the ground. Maintain excellent alignment during this workout. Similar to walking the plank, but on your side. You can stretch your free hand upward or place it on your hip. Whatever suits you best.

- Pro advice: If you find it simpler to begin the exercise with staggered feet, then do so. Your forearm, which you are pulling yourself up on, must align with your shoulder.

SIT-UPS

They resemble pushups. Of course, you have witnessed them in action. Nevertheless, just in case, here's how to do it properly: Your knees should be slightly raised and bent while you lay on the ground with your back towards the ground. Firmly plant your feet. The next step is to make a diamond shape with your arms, like in the bicycle crunches, by placing your hands behind your head.

You should breathe in when you stand up and out when lying back down. Take it gently and maintain control; speed does not necessarily indicate improved performance in this exercise. Keep your abdomen contracted and your back straight.

- Pro advice: Never use your arms to raise yourself. You should utilize your core muscles to carry out the job. The only way it will function for you is in that way. Your core is the only thing you want to move. The rest must remain precisely in place as you stand and sit back down. Furthermore, don't stand up from the ground.

GLUTE BRIDGE

Put yourself in a sit-up posture, but instead of putting your hands behind your back, keep them by your hips, palms facing up. Now that you are in this position, you want to merge it with the blank, so elevate your hips till a triangle is formed. Your legs, hips, and back should all be straight. Hold it for a few seconds before easing back down gradually.

- Pro advice: Do not exert heel pressure. You must support yourself by relying only on your hips.

FIRST WEEKLY WORKOUT PLAN

Day 1	Day 2	Day 3	Day 4
10 Jumping-Jacks 10 Push-ups 10 Squats	15 Sit-ups 10 Burpees 10 Lunges 30 Plank	15 Side planks 10 Crunches 15 Burpees	REST DAY
Day 5	**Day 6**	**Day 7**	
15 Sit-ups 15 Twisting Mountain climbers 15 Squats 40 Glute bridge	20 lunges 15 crunches 15 Burpees 30 Planks	25 squats 15 sit-ups 20 Crunches 60 Planks	

SECOND WEEKLY WORKOUT PLAN

DAY 1: Walk or run for at least 30/40 minutes at a brisk pace, enough to make you breath heavily but not breathless.

DAY 2: SHORT CIRCUIT

Perform a 5-minute warmup before starting the workout. You can choose between going for a quick run, skipping a rope, or doing 10 burpees and 20 jumping jacks.

MUSCLE GROUP	EXERCISE	REPS
DELTS/CHEST/TRICEP	PUSH-UP	10/20
LEGS	WALKING LUNGE	10 PER LEG
ABS	CRUNCH	20
DELTS/CHEST/BICEPS	BICEPS PUSH-UP	10/20
LEGS	BODYWEIGHT SQUAT	20
ABS	HIP TRUST	20

After each circuit, rest for 2 minutes. Repeat the circuit as many times as you can in 30 minutes.

DAY 3: DUMBELLS EXERCISES. You can use bottles of water or jugs of milk instead of dumbbells, using a weight that allows you to perform 2 sets of 12 reps of each exercise. Make sure you warm up before the workout with a 5-minute warm-up exercise.

-DEADLIFTS. Make sure you perform the exercise with your feet shoulder-width apart. You should also avoid any excessive curvature or rounding of your spine, especially in your lower back.

-SIDE LATERAL RAISES. When you lift your arms until they are parallel to the floor, hold for a second before returning to the starting position.

-OVERHEAD PRESS. You can press both arms at once or alternate them.

- **TRICEPS EXTENSIONS.** You can do this exercise lying on a bench or on the floor.

- **ARM CURLS.** Make sure you control the movement during the concentric and eccentric movements, focusing on the bicep's contraction.

- **BENCH PRESS.** You can also perform this exercise flat, lying on your exercise mat on the floor.

- **BENT OVER ROWS.** Make sure you bend 45 degrees from the waist, keep your back flat and chest open, and lift the weight by moving your arms back and squeezing your shoulder blades.

- **SHOULDER SQUAT.** Stand with your feet shoulder-width apart and hold your dumbbells above each shoulder.

DAY 4: Rest or walk/ run for 30 minutes at a brisk pace.

DAY 5: Repeat the day 2 short circuit.

DAY 6: Repeat the day 3 dumbbell exercise workout.

DAY 7: Rest.

MEASURING CONVERSION TABLE FROM AMERICAN TO EUROPEAN.

CUPS	TBSP	TSP	ONCE	ML
1 cup	16 tbsp	48 tsp	8 oz	237 ml
¾ cup	12 tbsp	36 tsp	6 oz	177 ml
⅔ cup	10 tbsp + 2 tsp	32 tsp	5 ⅓ oz	158 ml
½ cup	8 tbsp	24 tsp	4 oz	118 ml
⅓ cup	5 tbsp + 1 tsp	16 tsp	2 ⅔ oz	79 ml
¼ cup	4 tbsp	12 tsp	2 oz	59 ml

CONCLUSION

Thank you for making it to the end. Whether your cholesterol has crept up over the years or you have an inherited problem, a healthy diet can significantly impact your cholesterol levels and heart health. It will also improve your health in other ways, such as lowering blood pressure, preventing diabetes, and assisting you in maintaining a healthy weight.

Lowering cholesterol appears to be on everyone's mind these days. It's become a common topic of discussion, with articles about it in your local newspaper and television advertisements for treatments. Perhaps you're reading this book because your doctor declared your cholesterol "high" or "borderline." These phrases appear to be thrown around all the time.

Anyone with high cholesterol can benefit from adopting a heart-healthy, cholesterol-lowering lifestyle. Inadequate exercise and eating the wrong foods are two common causes of high cholesterol. A balanced lifestyle that includes exercise and eating heart-healthy foods, on the other hand, can naturally lower cholesterol.

However, it is important to remember that medications, such as statin medication, have a much higher success rate when prescribed than when used as self-administered supplements. Many people have tried to lower bad cholesterol through diet and exercise, but it is still very high in many cases. People must use diet choices effectively and efficiently to lower bad cholesterol and maintain a healthy weight.

All the best!

INDEX

A

Almond Noodles with Cauliflower; 150
Almond Rice Pudding with Raspberry Sauce; 179
Asian Chicken Breasts; 91
Avocado and Watermelon Mix; 40

B

Baked Fish Served with Vegetables; 127
Banana Cream and Lowfat Yogurt; 180
Basil Pesto; 167
Beef Veggie Pot Meal; 107
Beef with Mushrooms; 108
Bell Pepper Pancakes; 27
Berries Cobbler; 181
Berry, Walnut, and Cinnamon Quinoa Bowl; 36
Black Beans Burgers; 151
Braised Beef Shanks; 109
Buckwheat with Potatoes and Kale; 153
Butternut Squash, Lentils and Spinach Gratin; 154

C

Carrot Cake; 191
Cashew Pesto & Parsley with Veggies; 42
Cauliflower and Horseradish Soup; 66
Cauliflower Mashed "Potatoes"; 156
Cauliflower Sprinkled with Curry; 44
Cauliflower, Spinach and Sweet Potato Lasagna; 157
Cauliflower-Cream Pasta with Mint; 159
Celery and Chili Peppers Stir Fry; 45
Cheesy Zucchini Pancake; 176
Chicken and Quinoa Salad; 46
Chicken Thighs and Apples Mix; 92
Chicken Tikka; 92
Chicken Tortillas; 94
Chickpea Bowls with Tahini Sauce; 160
Chickpea Garlic Noodle Soup; 68
Chipotle Lime Avocado Salad; 48
Chocolate Chip Cookies; 183
Chocolate Cupcakes; 184
Cilantro Lime Salmon Bowls; 130
Cinnamon Baked Apple Chips; 186
Citrus Pork; 110
Classic Chicken Cooking With Tomatoes & Tapenade; 95
Coconut-Berry Sunrise Smoothie; 28
Collard Greens Dish; 65

Coriander Falafel; 174
Cream of Mushroom Soup; 69
Creamy chocolate-cherry smoothie; 29
Creamy Oats Banana Porridge; 39
Curry Lentil Soup; 71

D

Dates Cream; 187
Delicious Chicken Tenders; 96

E

Easy Basic Table Salad; 162
Easy Shrimp; 131
Easy strawberry kiwi smoothie; 30
Easy Veal Chops; 112
Edamame and Avocado Dip; 49
Eggplant Fries; 23

F

Flavors Vegetable Stew; 72
Flounder with Tomatoes and Basil; 133
Fruit Smoothie with Greek Yogurt; 31

G

Garlic and Tomatoes on Mussels; 134
Garlic Lime Marinated Pork Chops; 113
Garlic Lovers Hummus; 163
Garlic Mushroom Chicken; 97
Ginger and carrot pear smoothie; 32
Ginger Sesame Salmon; 135
Greek Lentil Soup; 74
Green Apple and Oat Bran Smoothie; 33
Green Goddess Crab Salad with Endive; 136
Green smoothie with berry and banana; 34
Grilled Cauliflower with Spicy Lentil Sauce; 164
Grilled Chicken; 99
Grilled Fennel-Cumin Lamb Chops; 114
Grilled Halibut and Fruit Salsa; 137

H

Healthy Beef cabbage; 115
Healthy Carrot Chips; 50
Healthy Cauliflower Purée; 165
Healthy Chicken Orzo; 100
Healthy Meatballs; 117
Hearty Brussels and Pistachio; 177
Hearty Pork Belly Casserole; 118

Hearty Vegetable Stew; 75
Homemade Guacamole; 51
Homemade Protein Bar; 187
Honey-Lime Berry Salad; 52
Hot Chicken Wings; 102

I

Indian Vegetable Stew; 77

J

Jerk Beef and Plantain Kabobs; 119
Juicy Chicken Patties; 103

L

Lamb Chops with Rosemary; 120
Lemon Broccoli; 24
Lentil Veggie Stew; 79

M

Mango Panna Cotta; 193
Mexican Lentil Soup; 80
Millet Porridge; 25
Muesli with Berries, Seeds, and Nuts; 35

N

Nuts And Seeds Trail Mix; 53

P

Pan fried Green Beans; 168
Pan-Grilled Fish Steaks; 139
Peach-Cranberry Sunrise Muesli; 38
Pesto Shrimp Pasta; 140
Pita Chips; 54
Pork Meatloaf; 122
Pork, Water Chestnuts, and Cabbage Salad; 123
Portobello Mushroom Stew; 82

Q

Quinoa Almond Porridge; 26

R

Rainbow Fruit Salad; 41
Ravaging Beef Pot Roast; 124
Roasted Broccoli Salad; 55

Roasted Chickpeas; 169
Roasted Eggplant Sandwiches; 170
Roasted Veggie and Lemon Pepper Salmon; 147
Root Vegetable Stew; 83

S

Salmon Avocado Salad; 141
Salmon with Dill and Lemon; 143
Salmon Wrap; 144
Sautéed Garlic Mushrooms; 57
Savory Chicken and Watermelon Rind Soup; 84
Shortbread Cookies; 189
Shrimp and Avocado Salad; 145
Simple Tuna and Cucumber Salad; 146
Slow Cooked Quinoa and Lentils Tacos; 171
Smoky Cauliflower; 58
Spicy Chicken; 104
Spicy Lentil Chili; 86
Stir-Fried Sesame Shrimp; 148
Strawberries and Amaretto Cream; 194
Stuffed Tex-Mex Baked Potatoes; 172
Sweet and Spicy Brussels Sprouts; 56
Sweet Carrots; 59

T

Tasty Chicken Wings; 105
Tasty Pork Patties; 125
Thick & Creamy Potato Soup; 88
Tofu with Brussels sprouts; 60
Tomato, Basil and Cucumber Salad; 61
Turmeric Peppers Platter; 63
Tuscan Fish Stew; 89

W

Walnut butter Bars; 190
White Beans with Spinach and Pan-Roasted Tomato; 173

Z

Zucchini Pizza Bites; 64

Printed in Great Britain
by Amazon